D0347917

RONALDO

MATT AND TOM OLDFIELD

CLASSIC
FOOTBALL HEROES

RONALDO

FROM THE PLAYGROUND
TO THE PITCH

DINO

Published by Dino Books
an imprint of John Blake Publishing
3 Bramber Court, 2 Bramber Road,
London W14 9PB, England

www.johnblakepublishing.co.uk

www.facebook.com/johnblakebooks
twitter.com/jblakebooks

This edition published in 2018

ISBN: 978 1 78606 944 3

All rights reserved. No part of this publication may be reproduced, stored in a
retrieval system, or transmitted in any form or by any means, without the prior
permission in writing of the publisher, nor be otherwise circulated in any form
of binding or cover other than that in which it is published and without a similar
condition including this condition being imposed on the subsequent purchaser.

British Library Cataloguing-in-Publication Data:

A catalogue record for this book is available from the British Library.

Design by www.envydesign.co.uk

Printed in Great Britain by Clays Ltd, St Ives plc

1 3 5 7 9 10 8 6 4 2

© Text copyright Matt and Tom Oldfield 2018

The right of Matt and Tom Oldfield to be identified as the authors of this
work has been asserted by them in accordance with the Copyright,
Designs and Patents Act 1988.

Papers used by John Blake Publishing are natural, recyclable products made from
wood grown in sustainable forests. The manufacturing processes conform to the
environmental regulations of the country of origin.

Every attempt has been made to contact the relevant copyright-holders, but some
were unobtainable. We would be grateful if the appropriate people could contact us.

John Blake Publishing is an imprint of Bonnier Publishing.
www.bonnierpublishing.co.uk

For Noah and Nico,
Southampton's future strikeforce

CLASSIC
FOOTBALL HEROES

Matt Oldfield is an accomplished writer and the editor-in-chief of football review site Of Pitch & Page. Tom Oldfield is a freelance sports writer and the author of biographies on Cristiano Ronaldo, Arsène Wenger and Rafael Nadal.

Cover illustration by Dan Leydon.
To learn more about Dan visit danleydon.com
To purchase his artwork visit etsy.com/shop/footynews
Or just follow him on Twitter @danleydon

TABLE OF CONTENTS

ACKNOWLEDGEMENTS

First of all, I'd like to thank John Blake Publishing – and particularly my editor James Hodgkinson – for giving me the opportunity to work on these books and for supporting me throughout. Writing stories for the next generation of football fans is both an honour and a pleasure.

I wouldn't be doing this if it wasn't for Tom. I owe him so much and I'm very grateful for his belief in me as an author. I feel like Robin setting out on a solo career after a great partnership with Batman. I hope I do him (Tom, not Batman) justice with these new books.

Next up, I want to thank my friends for keeping

9

me sane during long hours in front of the laptop. Pang, Will, Mills, Doug, John, Charlie – the laughs and the cups of coffee are always appreciated.

I've already thanked my brother but I'm also very grateful to the rest of my family, especially Melissa, Noah and of course Mum and Dad. To my parents, I owe my biggest passions: football and books. They're a real inspiration for everything I do.

Finally, I couldn't have done this without Iona's encouragement and understanding during long, work-filled weekends. Much love to you.

CHAPTER 1

WORLD CUP HERO

International Stadium, Yokohama, 30 June 2002
First 1994, then 1998, and now 2002. Ronaldo was
about to play in his third World Cup Final and this
one was going to be the best by far. As he looked
around at his amazing teammates in the tunnel,
Ronaldo was sure of it.

Cafu and Roberto Carlos, Ronaldinho and Rivaldo.
For the first time in years, Brazil had great defenders
and great attackers. It was their best team since
1982, and perhaps their best since 1970 and the
days of Pelé.

Back in 1994, Ronaldo had been 'The New Pelé',
an exciting seventeen-year-old striker who couldn't

stop scoring goals. At that tournament, he watched and waited but never got his chance. He collected a winners' medal, but it never felt like he'd earned it.

Four years later in France, Ronaldo was Brazil's superstar. He led them all the way to that 1998 final but, with the weight of the nation resting on his shoulders, he wasn't well enough to win the World Cup for his country. That's why 2002 meant so much to Ronaldo – it was his chance to make things right.

In 2000, a knee injury had looked like it might end his international career, but he never gave up. Thanks to lots of hard work, he bounced back, and in 2002 he was off to South Korea and Japan for Brazil's third World Cup Final in a row.

As they lined up on the pitch for the national anthems, Ronaldo and Ronaldinho shared a joke. Even minutes before a World Cup Final, they couldn't help laughing. That was the Brazilian way. Winning was, of course, really important, but so was having fun. The nation loved to see entertaining football. They called it 'o jogo bonito' – 'The Beautiful Game'.

As the Brazilian players took up their positions, however, their smiles disappeared. They were totally focused on bringing the World Cup trophy home for a record fifth time.

'Come on!' Ronaldo roared above the noise of 70,000 fans.

He was Brazil's big game player. He had shown it in the semi-final against Turkey and now it was time to show it in the final against Germany. They had lots of excellent, experienced players, but where were their superstars? There was no-one that could compete with 'The Three Rs' – Ronaldo, Rivaldo and Ronaldinho. At their best, they were in a league of their own.

Rivaldo passed to Ronaldinho, who threaded the ball through to Ronaldo. He just had Oliver Kahn in goal to beat. The Brazil fans jumped to their feet. When Ronaldo was one-on-one with the goalkeeper, there was usually only one result – goal.

This time, however, Ronaldo got his angles wrong, and the ball trickled harmlessly wide. He put his hands to his face.

'How did I miss that?' he cried out.

He didn't let it get him down, though. He knew that he would get more chances to score a World Cup Final goal.

At half-time, Ronaldo walked off the pitch shaking his head. Four times, he had shot at goal and four times, the ball hadn't gone in. He was supposed to be Brazil's star striker, but Kahn was winning their battle.

'Be patient,' manager Luiz Felipe Scolari told his players in the dressing room. 'There's no need to panic!'

In the second half, they came closer and closer to scoring until finally, the goal arrived.

Ronaldo chased back to win the ball off Dietmar Hamann. He passed to Rivaldo, who went for a quick long-range shot. It flew straight at Kahn in goal, but it was so powerful that he spilled it.

After his pass, Ronaldo had kept on running towards goal. If there was even the smallest chance of a rebound, he was there waiting to pounce. It was one of the simplest tap-ins of his career.

Gooooooooooooooooooaaaaaaaaaaaaaaaallllllllllll llllllllllllllll!!!!!!!!!!!!!!!!!!!!

Brazil had the lead and Ronaldo had his first World Cup Final goal. The whole team celebrated together.

Ronaldo was a little lucky with his first goal but there was nothing lucky about his second. As Kléberson passed the ball across, Rivaldo knew that Ronaldo was behind him. So, he went for the dummy and fooled Germany's last defender. Ronaldo took a touch and swept the ball right into the bottom corner.

Gooooooooooooooooooaaaaaaaaaaaaaaaallllllllllll llllllllllllllll!!!!!!!!!!!!!!!!!!!!

It was his eighth goal of the tournament, the highest number for over thirty years. Ronaldo had also doubled his total from 1998.

'We've done it!' he screamed with joy.

That's when the Brazilian carnival started. The stadium was a sea of yellow and green, and the fans danced in their seats to the sounds of the samba drums. They were minutes away from glory, seconds away…

On the subs bench, Ronaldo wrapped himself in the national flag and waited for the party to really begin. Finally, the referee blew the whistle. It was over, and Brazil were the World Champions.

Ronaldo was carried back on to the pitch on the shoulders of his teammates. After losing the 1998 final in Paris, he had returned to book his place in football history. Ronaldo was the latest in a long line of modern-day Brazilian footballing heroes that started with Pelé.

Success was a team effort, however. They formed a big circle on the pitch – the players, the coaches, the manager Scolari who had always believed in Ronaldo, and even the doctors who had helped with his recovery. They had all played a part in making their country proud.

When their captain Cafu kissed and lifted the World Cup, silver confetti flew up into the Japanese sky. The Brazilian players were all desperate to touch the trophy, but when Ronaldo walked forward, they stepped aside. This was his big moment.

'Here,' Gilberto Silva said, handing over the trophy to Ronaldo. 'Enjoy it, *O Fenomeno!*'

As 'The Phenomenon' raised it high, that famous toothy grin spread across his face. After years of expectation, Ronaldo had lived up to his full, amazing potential. It hadn't always been an easy journey but the Boy from Bento Ribeiro had followed his dream to become the best player in the world and Brazil's World Cup hero.

CHAPTER 2

THE BOY FROM BENTO RIBEIRO

'Have you decided on a name, Mrs de Lima?' the doctor asked.

Sônia shook her head. 'Sorry, I'm waiting for my husband. He's on his way.'

Where was Nélio Sr? What was taking him so long? Why wasn't he rushing over to meet his third child? In her hospital bed, Sônia held her newborn son in her arms and panicked.

'What's your name?' she asked the doctor.

'Ronaldo Valente,' he replied.

Ronaldo – Sônia liked the name. If it was good enough for a doctor, then it was good enough for her son. She was determined to do everything possible to give him a bright future. A witch doctor had told her that her second son would be born with amazing gifts that would help the family escape from poverty. Looking down at his face, he certainly looked like a healthy little boy. Perhaps with the right name, he would now go on and become a great doctor.

'We'll call him Ronaldo,' Sônia announced.

The doctor looked surprised. 'It would be an honour, but are you sure?'

This time, Sônia nodded her head. She was too tired to think of any other names.

Eventually, Nélio Sr arrived to take Sônia and baby Ronaldo back home. Home was a house in Bento Ribeiro, one of the poorest parts of Rio de Janeiro. It wasn't easy bringing up a young family in Brazil. It was hard to find good jobs, and Nélio Sr and Sônia now had three hungry mouths to feed.

Ione and Nélio Jr were so excited to meet their new brother.

'Careful!' their mum reminded them. 'He's not a toy.'

With his siblings chasing him around and his

parents often away at work, Ronaldo grew up fast. He had lots and lots of energy to use up, and it wasn't long before he was walking, and then running. Speaking, however, wasn't so easy. Ronaldo was a quiet child and it didn't help that his own name was quite difficult to say.

'Try again,' his sister Ione said. 'Who are you?'

'Dadado,' he spluttered.

'No, Ron-al-do.'

'Da-da-do.'

Nélio Jr laughed. 'Let's just call him Dadado. I like that name better anyway!'

For his fourth birthday, Ronaldo got the greatest gift a child can get – his first-ever football. As Nélio Sr handed it to him, his son's eyes lit up. Ronaldo had seen lots of kids playing with one in the streets, he had kicked one around with his brother lots of times, but now he had a football of his own. For the first few hours, he protected it like a valuable jewel.

'Shall we play?' Nélio Jr asked. He tried to slap the ball out of his brother's hands, but Ronaldo had a tight grip on it.

'No, it's mine!' he said fiercely.

'I know, but you're meant to kick it, not just hold it. It's called *foot*ball, not *hand*ball!'

Soon enough, Ronaldo realised that it wasn't that much fun just to carry the ball around like a teddy bear, or a favourite blanket. When his brother wasn't looking, he dropped it in front of his feet and then kicked it as hard as he could. *Bang!*

'What's that noise?' Sônia cried out. 'Nélio Jr? Ronaldo? Ione? You better not be breaking things!'

Luckily, Ronaldo's first big kick hadn't caused any damage. Nélio Jr giggled and put a finger to his lips. 'Shhhhhhhhhh – you've got to be careful, little man!'

Their game soon moved outside. It was best for everyone. Nélio Jr put down two rocks as goalposts and stood in the middle. 'Go on, shoot!'

Ione and Ronaldo took it in turns. Nélio Jr saved the first few, but he could see that his brother was getting frustrated. 'I better give him a chance,' Nélio Jr thought to himself.

Ronaldo swung back his right leg and *Bang!* The

ball flew towards the goal and somehow, it slipped through his brother's fingers.

Goooooooooooooooooooaaaaaaaaaaaaaaaallllllllllll llllllllllllll!!!!!!!!!!!!!!!!!!!!

'*Dadadoooooooo!*' Ione screamed, lifting her brother into the air.

'Noooooooooooo!' Nélio Jr screamed, pretending to be upset.

A huge smile spread across Ronaldo's face. He raised his little arms up into the sky. 'Let's do that again!' he cheered.

After a while, his brother and sister got bored and went back inside. Ronaldo, however, wasn't ready to stop. What football fun could he have on his own?

First, he just kicked the ball against a fence – right foot, then left foot, then right foot, then left foot. The more he practised, the more Ronaldo's control improved. He could happily do that for hours.

Sometimes, however, he let his imagination run wild. Their house was small but there was lots of land around it. It was all space for him to explore. With the ball at his feet, the fruit trees became big, tall, scary defenders. Ronaldo raced around at top speed, dribbling past all of them.

'*Dadadoooooooo!*' he screamed as he scored another wondergoal.

'I'm going to be the greatest football player ever,' Ronaldo thought to himself as he rushed inside for dinner. Even a superstar had to take a break to eat.

CHAPTER 3

FOOTBALL ALL DAY, EVERY DAY

As soon as his parents would let him, Ronaldo moved on from dribbling past fruit trees in the garden to dribbling past real opponents in the street.

'Look after your brother!' Sônia shouted to Nélio Jr as they raced out of the door.

Ronaldo played football all day, every day. It was his favourite thing to do. The street matches started early in the morning before school and only ended when it was too dark to see the ball and their stomachs were rumbling loudly.

As one of the youngest kids in the neighbourhood, Ronaldo had to earn the respect of his teammates first. He worked hard to win the ball for his team. When he got it, he kept things simple and tried not to show off too much. It was only after a few months that he felt confident enough to open up his full box of tricks.

There was never much space on their 'pitch', so it was all about clever footwork. Thanks to all that kicking against the fence, Ronaldo had two very clever feet to work with. He could dribble and shoot with his left and right, which made it very difficult for defenders. Which way would he go?

And that wasn't his only talent on the football field.

'I reckon you're quicker with the ball than without it!'

'Your balance is amazing. If I tried that many stepovers, I'd fall over for sure!'

'Where does all that power come from? No offence, but you're not exactly a big guy!'

Ronaldo laughed and shrugged. Just as the witch doctor had predicted, he had been born with amazing gifts. On his happy way home for dinner, he practised his keepy-uppies:

Ten with his right foot,

Ten with his left foot,

Ten with his left knee,

Ten with his right knee,

Ten with his head.

Controlling the ball on the back of his neck, he flicked it up into the air and juggled it on his right foot again.

'More, more!' Local people had stopped to watch the show and they clapped loudly. Ronaldo bowed and waved. He loved to entertain.

In between the street matches, Ronaldo went to school, but that didn't mean the football stopped. At first, some of his classmates made fun of his big front teeth and picked him last in the lunchtime games. That hurt Ronaldo's feelings but once he got the ball at his feet on the playground, the jokes soon ended.

'Wow, you're amazing!' they cried out. 'How did you do that?'

Suddenly, everyone wanted Ronaldo on their team. He was the best player in the school and also, now, the most popular. Not for the last time, football had saved the day.

In the few moments when he wasn't playing football, Ronaldo was most likely watching it. Nélio Sr often took his sons along to support his favourite team Flamengo at the massive Maracanã Stadium.

'That could be you guys one day!' he said as the players ran out onto the pitch.

Nélio Jr was a good player, but it was Ronaldo who had the special passion and the special talent. His dad had high hopes for his footballing future.

Ronaldo loved every second of the experience. The atmosphere, the songs and, of course, the skills. There was one player in particular who caught his eye, a player who was running rings around everyone.

'Who's the Number 10?' he asked his dad. 'I like him – he's awesome!'

Nélio Sr smiled proudly. 'You've got good taste, son! That's Zico, one of the best footballers I've ever seen.'

'I'm going to be like Zico when I'm older,' Ronaldo announced confidently.

'I believe in you!' his dad replied.

Normally, Ronaldo preferred playing football rather than watching it, but World Cups were special. Every four years, the whole Brazilian nation cheered their team to victory.

In 1982, Ronaldo and his friends started the preparations early. The people of Bento Ribeiro had their own tournament tradition. The locals bought lots of yellow, green and blue paint and covered the neighbourhood in bright colours. Everywhere you looked, there were national flags, birds, even murals of the football heroes.

'Look Dad, it's Zico!' Ronaldo pointed.

They watched every match together on their neighbour's TV. Not only did Mr Renato invite them in but he also gave them chips and Coca-Cola.

'You're the best neighbour ever!' Ronaldo cheered happily.

With Zico and Sócrates in midfield, Brazil scored lots of goals and won lots of matches. They weren't the only samba stars, though. Against the Soviet Union, Isidoro passed infield, Falcão dummied it and Éder flicked the ball up and volleyed it home.

'Look at that – o jogo bonito at its best!' Mr Renato said as they all celebrated.

'What does that mean?' Ronaldo asked.

'It means "The Beautiful Game". When Brazilians play football, it's a joy to watch. So much skill and flair. We're the best in the world!'

In 1982, however, they suffered a shock 3–2 defeat to Italy and didn't even reach the semi-finals. The whole country was in shock. Football was such an important part of Brazilian life. It was usually a source of pride for the people, but not after that.

'It's a tragedy!' Nélio Sr moaned. 'We were the top team in the tournament.'

Ronaldo felt upset too, but he also felt inspired. Watching his World Cup heroes in action, he thought, 'Maybe one day that could be me!'

No, he didn't think; he believed. Brazil would

soon need new World Cup heroes. What they would need most of all was a superstar striker who could shoot them all the way to glory.

'That's going to be me!' Ronaldo told himself.

CHAPTER 4

VALQUIERE TENNIS CLUB

As Sônia handed her son his lunchbox, she looked at him sternly. 'If I hear that you've been skipping school again, there's going to be big trouble. Do you understand me?'

Ronaldo looked down at his feet guiltily. 'Yes, Mamãe.'

'I know how much you love football, but your education is important too. Don't you want a bright future?'

'Yes, Mamãe.'

'Good, then go to class and learn! The games can wait until after school.'

Ronaldo didn't like to upset his mum, but he

was 100 per cent focused on his football education. There was so much to learn at the beaches of Rio de Janeiro.

Compared to the street football Ronaldo was used to, it was a totally different world. For the first time, he played on pitches with marked lines. Rather than twenty-a-side crowded chaos, only five players were allowed on each team. Instead of stones or jumpers, there were small goals with actual nets. It was amazing.

Ronaldo had the samba skills, but did he have the fitness? Running on sand all day turned out to be really hard work.

'School is a walk in the park compared to this!' he panted as sweat dripped down his face and soaked his T-shirt.

Nothing, however, could stop Ronaldo's star from shining. He was soon the best player around.

Once they had conquered beach football, Ronaldo and his friends moved on to Brazil's next favourite sport – futsal. It was indoor five-a-side football but with a smaller, heavier ball.

'Cool, sounds like fun!' Ronaldo cheered. He was always looking for new challenges, especially if they involved kicking a round ball.

Despite the name, Valquiere Tennis Club was actually a futsal club. Ronaldo had joined at the age of nine but unfortunately, they didn't have space for a new striker at the time. The only position available was in goal.

'Sure, why not?' Ronaldo shrugged happily. It was better than not playing at all.

At first, he enjoyed being a keeper but saving goals just wasn't as exciting as scoring them. He didn't give up, though. He kept going, hoping that he would eventually get the chance to show off his outfield skills.

Against league leaders Vasco da Gama, Valquiere were losing 2–0 at half-time. It looked like another game lost, so their coach decided to make some changes.

'Ronie, you'll be our striker in the second half,' Marquinhos announced. He had heard good things about the boy's technique and besides, he couldn't be any worse than his teammates. What did they have to lose?

Ronaldo's face lit up as he punched the air. This was the moment that he had been waiting for. The Vasco defenders, however, had no idea what was about to happen.

As soon as he got the ball, Ronaldo attacked at speed. He was a futsal natural. He moved it quickly from one foot to the other, daring his opponents to dive in for the tackle. With a stepover and a drop of the shoulder, he left the first defender behind.

Olé!

Ronaldo wanted to shoot but the goal was too far away. In futsal, you couldn't just hoof the ball from one end of the court to the other. You had to dribble or pass, and there wasn't much space for dribbling. So as the next defenders rushed towards him, Ronaldo chose to pass, and then move. He wanted the ball back as quickly as possible.

'One-two!' he called out to his teammate, who fed it through to him.

Ronaldo burst past the last defender and

suddenly he was one-on-one with the keeper. In the local street football matches, he was famous for his cool finishing. What would he do now? He pulled his right leg back as if he was going to hit the ball really hard. But then, as the goalkeeper started to dive, he side-footed the ball through his legs. Nutmeg!

Gooooooooooooooooooooaaaaaaaaaaaaaaaaaallllllllllll llllllllllllll!!!!!!!!!!!!!!!!!!!!!

The Valquiere players ran and jumped on their goalscoring hero. Ronaldo grinned back at them, but he didn't go wild. His team was still losing. There would be plenty of time for celebrations afterwards.

'Come on!' he roared.

The match became Ronaldo vs Vasco. Who would win?

Ronaldo scored: 2–2!

Vasco came back fighting: 3–2, 4–2!

Ronaldo got his hat-trick: 4–3!

Ronaldo set up his teammate: 4–4!

Ronaldo scored the matchwinner: 5–4!

At the final whistle, Valquiere celebrated a famous

victory. Marquinhos lifted his new star striker into the air.

'I think we're going to need to find a new goalkeeper!' he laughed.

Before long, however, Valquiere would also need to find a new striker. Fernando dos Santos Carvalho was in the crowd that day, watching Ronaldo's masterclass. Fernando was always on the lookout for the best young football talent. There were lots of skilful players around the city of Rio, but this kid looked very special indeed.

Fernando invited Ronaldo to join Social Ramos, a bigger and better futsal team. First, though, he had to get Sônia's permission.

'Training will be on Tuesdays and Thursdays,' Fernando explained when he visited the family home. 'I will pick your son up and take him on the bus to Social Ramos. How does that sound, Mrs de Lima?'

Sônia smiled. 'It sounds like my son will be safe and well looked after. Thank you, Mr Carvalho.'

On the bus to Social Ramos, what do you think

Ronaldo and Fernando talked about? Football, of course! Ronaldo was still a quiet, shy boy, but not when it came to his favourite subject. He could talk for hours about Zico, Flamengo and the Brazilian national team.

'I'm going to play in the World Cup one day,' Ronaldo told Fernando at one point.

With 166 goals in his first season, that didn't seem like a crazy dream at all.

CHAPTER 5

SÃO CRISTÓVÃO

After that record-breaking season, Ronaldo was
on the move again, from futsal to football. He was
heading for the big time. When Flamengo heard
about the thirteen-year-old goal machine, they
offered him a trial, much to the delight of his dad.

'I knew it!' Nélio Sr said proudly. 'My son is going
to be the next Zico!'

Ronaldo was thrilled about that idea too. On the
day of the trial, he woke up early to make the long
bus journey across Rio, from Bento Ribeiro to Gávea.
It wasn't easy on his own, but when it came to
football, Ronaldo was so determined.

Even when he arrived and saw Flamengo's

amazing training facilities, Ronaldo didn't get nervous. He believed in himself and his special talent. He was capable of anything and everything, and he showed that at the trial.

'Well done today,' the youth coach said to him afterwards. 'We'd like you to come back again tomorrow, if that's okay.'

'Yes!' Ronaldo thought to himself, but then he remembered one problem.

'I'm afraid I don't have enough money to take the bus again tomorrow,' he admitted with embarrassment. 'Is there any chance that I could borrow a few pennies and pay you back next week?'

'I'm really sorry but we can't do that.'

Ronaldo pleaded with the coach, but it was no use. The young star was devastated. How could they take away his football dream like that? He tried his best to find the money, but he didn't have enough time. When he didn't turn up to the second trial, Flamengo gave up on him.

Luckily, another club gave him a chance. Ary Ferreiras de Sá was a coach at São Cristóvão and he was looking for top new players to join the squad. Would Ronaldo be interested in playing for them?

'Of course!' he replied straight away.

São Cristóvão was much closer to home, which meant a much cheaper bus fare. This was Ronaldo's chance to put his Flamengo disaster behind him and start again. With his friend Calango at his side, he was ready to shine.

Ary knew all about the boy's amazing season at Social Ramos, but eleven-a-side football was very different from five-a-side futsal. Would Ronaldo be able to adapt to a bigger ball on a bigger, outdoor, grass pitch?

He looked so shy and skinny but as soon as he started playing, he seemed to grow in size and confidence like The Incredible Hulk.

Together, Ronaldo and Calango were a deadly duo, terrorising their opponents again and again. Calango looked very good, but Ronaldo looked exceptional. He had everything a top striker needed – speed, skill, strength, and a great eye for goal. He even played with a smile on his face, as if it was just a casual kickaround in the park.

'Wow, that kid is from another football planet!' Ary thought to himself.

On his São Cristóvão debut, Ronaldo scored a hat-trick, and that was just the beginning. He tore through defence after defence like a beast on the loose. Once he got the ball, it was game over. He dribbled towards goal with it stuck to his foot and no-one could stop him.

During Ronaldo's second season, a famous new coach arrived at the club. Jairzinho had been one of the heroes of Brazil's World Cup-winning team in 1970. He had played alongside Pelé, the King of Football.

Ronaldo couldn't wait to learn from Jairzinho and impress him with his talent. That didn't take long at all. Even in the very first training session, Ronaldo's star quality shone.

'Who's that?' Jairzinho asked Ary, pointing.

'That's Ronaldo.'

'Ronaldo,' São Cristóvão's new coach nodded his

head approvingly. He would make sure to remember that name. 'That boy's a bit special!'

He was right about that. Ronaldo had scored seventeen goals in twenty-eight games and he wasn't even the team's penalty taker. After one more successful season, the sixteen-year-old needed a new, tougher challenge. If he wanted to be a top professional footballer, it was time to join a top professional football club.

Ronaldo thanked everyone at São Cristóvão for all their help and support. 'I'll miss you guys,' he said as he left the training ground for the last time, 'and I'll never forget you!'

'Make sure you send us your shirt when you make your debut for Brazil!' Ary joked.

Ronaldo had signed for Cruzeiro, Jairzinho's old team. They needed a new star striker because Éder had finally retired.

'Wow, I remember watching his amazing goal at the 1982 World Cup,' Ronaldo said. 'I've got some very big boots to fill!'

'Good luck,' Jairzinho replied, 'although I really

don't think you'll need it!'

Belo Horizonte was only a five-hour drive from Bento Ribeiro, but to Ronaldo's young mind, it seemed like the other side of the world. Although he was nervous about leaving home, he was also excited about his next adventure.

'Good luck, son!' Sónia called out as she waved goodbye.

'Don't mess this up, bro!' Nélio Jr teased.

'I won't!' Ronaldo promised. He was off on his journey to become Brazil's next big superstar.

CHAPTER 6

CRUZEIRO

Even if Belo Horizonte didn't feel like home, at least the football pitch always did. It was where Ronaldo belonged and where he was happiest. As soon as he had a ball at his feet, everything else was forgotten. In his head, he was back in Bento Ribeiro, playing 'The Beautiful Game' in the streets with his friends.

In his first game for the Cruzeiro youth team, Ronaldo scored four times. As the goals kept flooding in, he moved up to the Reserves and then started training with the first team. The Cruzeiro Juniors won the Championship and Ronaldo was their top scorer. His talent was the talk of the town. Who was this young wizard and how soon would he be playing for the senior team?

When Cruzeiro got to the semi-finals of the Brazil Cup, their manager Pinheiro decided to rest many of his key players in the league matches. Which youngsters were ready to step up and take their places?

'Ronaldo!' the fans shouted.

Pinheiro listened and gave Ronaldo his debut against Caldense. He couldn't believe it. It was all happening so fast. He was still only sixteen and yet he was about to play professional football in front of thousands of cheering fans.

In the dressing room before kick-off, Ronaldo sat awkwardly in silence as his teammates chatted and laughed. Some of the more experienced players thought that it was because he was really nervous.

'Don't worry, you'll be fine,' full-back Paulo Roberto reassured him.

But Ronaldo wasn't nervous at all; he was just shy.

'Thanks,' he replied with a relaxed smile. 'I can't wait to play!'

Although he didn't score against Caldense,

Ronaldo didn't stay goalless for long. He was learning and improving with every minute on the pitch.

In the Copa Libertadores, Chilean team Colo-Colo felt the full force of Ronaldo's power. As Paulo crossed the ball in from the right, he made a late sprint into the six-yard box and tapped it in.

Goooooooooooooooooooooaaaaaaaaaaaaaaaaaallllllllllll llllllllllllllll!!!!!!!!!!!!!!!!!!!!

'Get in!' Ronaldo screamed, punching the air in delight as he ran over to hug Paulo.

Just before half-time, Ronaldo scored his second goal, but could he get a third to complete his first professional hat-trick? Of course, he could!

In the last minute of the match, the Cruzeiro left winger curled the ball into the danger zone. Ronaldo was alert and beat the Colo-Colo centre-back in the air. He flicked the ball down into the bottom corner.

Goooooooooooooooooooooaaaaaaaaaaaaaaaaaallllllllllll llllllllllllllll!!!!!!!!!!!!!!!!!!!!

Ronaldo had done it! He sank to his knees on the edge of the penalty area. The Cruzeiro fans clapped and cheered their amazing new Number 9.

Three goals in one match was a great achievement but Ronaldo knew he could do better. Against Bahía, he had a brilliant hat-trick before half-time.

'I want more!' Ronaldo cheered greedily.

His fourth goal was a penalty and his fifth was the icing on the cake. The Bahía goalkeeper dropped the ball as he moaned at his defenders. Out of nowhere, Ronaldo pounced, stole it and scored!

The match had been shown live on Brazilian TV and a new national star was born.

'I hope you recorded all of my goals!' Ronaldo grinned into the video camera.

He was a born entertainer. As he left the pitch, a crowd of people swarmed around him.

'You better get used to this!' Paulo warned him.

He was right. The Brazilian newspapers gave Ronaldo two new nicknames. The first was 'O Fenomeno' – 'The Phenomenon'. The second was 'The New Pelé'.

'Wow, that's a lot to live up to!' Ronaldo admitted.

Although he enjoyed the special attention, he kept his feet on the ground. He treated himself to a brand new car, but he sent most of his money home to his family in Bento Ribeiro. Just like the witch doctor had predicted, Ronaldo was helping them to escape from poverty.

He kept working hard in training, looking for ways to become an even better striker. He practised headers for hours with Paulo and the Cruzeiro goalkeeper, Dida. He wanted to be able to score from any angle and any distance.

'Okay, I'm going home now!' Dida shouted eventually, ripping his gloves off.

Ronaldo laughed. 'That's what my brother used to say when we were younger!'

It wasn't just the Brazilians who were impressed with the young striker's performances. All of Europe's top clubs sent scouts to watch Ronaldo play. Suddenly, Cruzeiro received offers from Portugal, England, Germany and Italy. Their offers started at £500,000 and quickly rose to £3 million.

But Cruzeiro said, 'No, we want £7 million!'

That transfer fee would make Ronaldo the most expensive player in Brazilian football history. In

1993, that was a huge amount of money, especially for a seventeen-year-old.

'Maybe next year,' the clubs decided.

Ronaldo was in no rush. He had plenty of time to go and play in Europe. For now, he was enjoying himself in his home country. With twenty-two goals in eighteen games, Ronaldo led Cruzeiro all the way to the league title. He was a scoring machine.

'Do you think you can reach the Brazilian squad?' a journalist asked him.

'It's early days,' Ronaldo replied, 'but I'd love to get the chance to represent my country.'

Ronaldo was being modest. His childhood dream was about to come true.

CHAPTER 7

BRAZIL'S NEXT BIG STAR

Ahead of the 1994 World Cup, Brazil's national team coach Carlos Alberto Parreira thought long and hard about his squad. He had plenty of talented and experienced players in every position – Cláudio Taffarel in goal, Aldair in defence, Dunga and Raí in midfield, and Bebeto and Romário in attack. Brazil had a strong line-up but there was one thing missing – a young player with flair.

'I want a wild card in my squad,' Parreira told his coaches. 'At the World Cup, we'll need to have a Plan B on the bench, something different to change the game. What I'm looking for is an exciting young forward with lots of speed and skill. Any ideas?'

There were two main candidates – a twenty-one-year-old winger playing for Corinthians and a seventeen-year-old striker playing for Cruzeiro. The first was called Rivaldo and the second was, of course, Ronaldo.

'The kid has scored forty-four goals in forty-seven games,' one coach explained enthusiastically. 'He's going to be Brazil's Next Big Star!'

'He was also brilliant for the Under-17s on their US tour,' added another. 'He scored five goals in three games.'

Parreira listened carefully and made a decision. 'Right, let's see what both of them can do!'

In March 1994, Brazil faced their South American rivals Argentina in a friendly match. It was the perfect time to give new young players a chance to shine.

Ronaldo was in shock when he heard the news. He had played a few times for the Brazil Under-17s but never for the Under-21s, or even the Under-19s. Now, he was going straight into the senior squad.

'This is crazy!' he told his dad.

Nélio Sr smiled and hugged his son. 'Don't let it faze you. This is what you were born to do. Good luck!'

Raí and Bebeto started the game in Recife but Rivaldo and Ronaldo were there on the bench, ready and waiting.

'How are you feeling, kid?' Rivaldo grinned, wearing the famous yellow-and-green shirt with Number 21 on the back.

Next to him, Ronaldo wore Number 19. He looked up at the 85,000 supporters in the stadium and remembered his father's advice. 'Good!' he laughed, looking really relaxed.

Rivaldo came on at half-time but not Ronaldo. He kept watching and waiting on the sidelines. As the second half flew by, he began to lose hope of making his international debut. But then, after seventy-five minutes, Bebeto scored to make it 2–0 to Brazil. Game over! Ronaldo dared to dream again.

'Hopefully they'll bring me on now,' he thought to himself.

His wish came true. With ten minutes to go, Parreira brought Ronaldo on for Bebeto.

'Go show them what you can do!' Bebeto, Brazil's great goalscorer, told Ronaldo as he left the field.

Ronaldo nodded confidently. That was his plan.

Most young players like to settle in with a safe, simple pass. Ronaldo, however, wasn't most young players. His first touch as a Brazilian international was a backheel flick! An Argentina defender blocked it, but that still didn't stop him from trying his tricks.

Fouling didn't stop Ronaldo either. He was only on the pitch for ten minutes, but that was enough time to receive some heavy, frustrated tackles. It was Argentina's only answer to his fancy footwork. Every time he fell, Ronaldo picked himself up, pulled his socks up, and carried on. If he wasn't calling for the ball, he was chasing after it. He was having the time of his life.

'Well played,' Parreira said at the final whistle. 'You were like a tornado out there!'

The Brazil manager was impressed. Had he found his World Cup wildcard? Perhaps, but Parreira needed to see more than just the last ten minutes of a match. What could Ronaldo do in the full ninety minutes? In their next friendly against Iceland, he was named in the starting line-up.

Ronaldo couldn't wait. The World Cup was only weeks away now and this was his last chance to impress. He was desperate to be on that plane to the USA.

'I just need a goal,' he told himself. He was wearing Number 7 – Bebeto's shirt. Hopefully, it would bring him good luck.

Paulo Sérgio ran forward from midfield and played the ball into Ronaldo. He used his strength to hold off the defender and then his skill to flick it on for the one-two.

Olé!

As Paulo dribbled into the penalty area, he was tackled but the ball bounced out to Ronaldo. Without even thinking, he took a shot. After a deflection off Paulo's heels, it landed in the bottom corner.

*Goooooooooooooooooooooaaaaaaaaaaaaaaaaalllllllllllll
llllllllllllllll!!!!!!!!!!!!!!!!!!!!!*

Ronaldo raised his arms to the sky. He was off the mark in international football! Or was he?

'Wasn't that my goal?' Paulo teased him as they celebrated together.

Ronaldo shook his head fiercely. He took scoring very seriously. 'No way, that's mine! It was going in anyway.'

'RONALDOOOOOOOOOOOOOOOOOOOOOOO!' boomed out the crowd in the stadium as one voice.

He turned to Paulo and smiled. 'See!'

Ronaldo didn't score Brazil's second goal, but he created it with his skill. As he dribbled into the penalty area at top speed, he changed direction, moving the ball beautifully from the right to the left. It was a switch that totally fooled the Iceland centre-back. Penalty!

'Great work!' Mazinho cheered as he helped the young star up off the grass.

Ronaldo was involved in his team's third goal too. Late in the second half, he chased after a long ball and, of course, he won the race. The keeper saved his shot, but Viola was there for the rebound.

RONALDO

On the pitch, the Brazil players hugged each other.
In the stands, the Brazil supporters danced as one
big yellow mass. And on the touchline, the Brazil
manager clapped and smiled. He was watching a
seventeen-year-old put on a striking masterclass.
Ronaldo had everything – strength, skill *and* speed.
Parreira had found his World Cup wildcard.

CHAPTER 8

WORLD CUP 1994

There was lots of excitement in Brazil as they waved
their national team off to the 1994 World Cup in
the USA. Back in 1990, they had suffered a shock
1–0 defeat to Argentina in the second round of the
tournament, but this time Brazil had bounced back
better and stronger. They had a new star strikeforce
of Romário and Bebeto, plus a new young wildcard
up their sleeve.

'Do you think Ronaldo will play?' the Brazilian
people wondered.

Some thought he would be used as a super sub,
while others thought he was just going along for
the experience. Whatever the answer, Ronaldo was

following in the footsteps of another seventeen-year-old Brazilian – Pelé, The King of Football. In 1958, Pelé won the World Cup for his country and he even scored two goals in the final. That was a lot for Ronaldo to live up to.

'There will never be another Pelé,' Parreira said, trying to calm things down. 'We have five strikers and Ronaldo is one of them. Any of them could play.'

Ronaldo wasn't worried about the pressure, though. He never let the talk bother him. On the training ground, he focused on doing everything possible to force his way into the team. He was a lot younger than all of his teammates, so young that he was still wearing braces on his teeth.

But on the ball, Ronaldo showed no fear or respect. He just did what he always did – torment defenders with his powerful running and quick feet.

'He's like an express train!' Aldair complained.

Romário and Bebeto, however, upped their game. They were Brazil's stars and they weren't going to let a teenager steal their World Cup starting spots.

In their first match against Russia, Romário and

Raí got the goals. With Brazil winning 2–0, Parreira decided to protect the lead. He brought on defensive players, not attackers.

Wearing the Number 20 shirt, Ronaldo jumped up to celebrate each goal with the rest of the squad. It was important to be a good team player. He tried his best to stay patient but that wasn't easy for a seventeen-year-old who just wanted to play football. One opportunity – that was all he was looking for.

With a 3–0 victory over Cameroon, Brazil qualified for the second round, and they still had one group game left against Sweden.

'Maybe the manager will rest some of the stars for this one!' Ronaldo wondered hopefully.

Sadly, Parreira stuck with the same strong team, which meant that Ronaldo was left on the bench again.

He stayed there against the Netherlands, even when it was 2–2 with ten minutes to go.

And he stayed there against Sweden, even when it was 0–0 with ten minutes to go.

The Brazil fans always wanted to win, of course,

but they wanted to win with their unique football
style. Their teams were famous for playing 'The
Beautiful Game'. Pelé and Garrincha, Zico and
Sócrates – they were all born entertainers. At the
1994 World Cup, however, Brazil went for tactics
over talent. With so much boring defending, where
had 'The Beautiful Game' gone? Their fans cried out
for Ronaldo's flair but Parreira didn't listen.

'Why doesn't he trust me?' Ronaldo asked his dad
on the phone. He was becoming more and more
frustrated. 'If the manager's not going to play me,
why did he bring me here?'

'To watch and learn,' Nélio Sr tried to explain, but
his son didn't want to hear it.

'I can do my learning out on the pitch!' Ronaldo
replied.

In the World Cup Final, Brazil were up against
Italy, the best defenders in the world. Franco Baresi
and Paolo Maldini knew all about Romário and
Bebeto. They used their strength and intelligence to
keep the skilful attackers very quiet.

'Yes, but they don't know about *me!*' Ronaldo

wanted to tell his manager. Wasn't that why Parreira had brought him to the World Cup in the first place – to be Brazil's wildcard, their Plan B? He was desperate to get out there and use his pace, power and skill to cause problems.

But it was Viola who came on to replace Zinho in extra-time, not Ronaldo. Ronaldo slumped back in his seat. He wasn't going to be a World Cup hero this time.

'Never mind, I'll just have to make sure that there's a next time,' Ronaldo told himself.

When Brazil won the penalty shoot-out, he sprinted over to join the big team celebrations. He swapped shirts with Italy's Pierluigi Casiraghi and draped his country's flag around his shoulders. He collected his winner's medal and he kissed the World Cup trophy.

Campeones, Campeones, Olé Olé Olé!

It was a joyful night for all Brazilians, but Ronaldo was far from satisfied. He hadn't done anything to deserve the medal around his neck. He hadn't played a single minute of football. Being there in the

USA was a great experience for a young player, but Ronaldo wanted to be involved. He wanted to feel like he had helped to make his nation proud.

'You'll get your chance, kid,' Romário said, putting an arm around Ronaldo's shoulder. Romário was twenty-eight years old and Bebeto was already thirty. 'By the time the 1998 World Cup comes around, you're going to be the star!'

CHAPTER 9

PSV: THE NEW ROMÁRIO

In the 1990s, when young Brazilian stars decided to leave their homeland, they didn't usually go straight to the world's top teams. Instead, they went to the Dutch or French leagues, to learn more about European football first. Big clubs like AC Milan and Juventus wanted to sign Ronaldo, but was he ready to go straight in at the highest level?

His international teammate Romário had spent five seasons at PSV Eindhoven before moving on to Barcelona. The Dutch club were now looking for a special young striker to replace him.

'You'd be perfect!' Romário told him excitedly. 'It's a great club with great coaches. Once you get used to the style of football, you'll be scoring goals for fun!'

Ronaldo liked the sound of that and decided to take his friend's advice. Once he returned from the 1994 World Cup, he left Cruzeiro to join PSV for £5 million. That was a big transfer fee for a little-known seventeen-year-old, but it soon turned out to be an absolute bargain.

Ronaldo made his Dutch league debut in the first match of the season against Vitesse Arnhem. As he ran out onto the pitch wearing the Number 9 shirt, the PSV fans clapped loudly. They couldn't wait to watch 'the new Romário' in action.

After ten minutes, Ronaldo ran onto a great longball from his strike partner, Luc Nilis. He took one touch and slotted the ball calmly past the goalkeeper.

Goooooooooooooooooooooaaaaaaaaaaaaaaaaaallllllllllll llllllllllllllll!!!!!!!!!!!!!!!!!

'Welcome to the club!' his new teammates cheered, hugging him one by one.

'*Dank je!*' Ronaldo said, high-fiving Luc for the

assist. 'Thank you' was all he could say in Dutch so far, but he would soon learn the language.

In the second half, Ronaldo returned the favour. He played a great pass through to Luc, who made it 4–2 to PSV.

Ronaldo was off to a flying start and once he settled in Eindhoven, he got better and better. Against Bayer Leverkusen in the UEFA Cup, PSV were 4–1 down after forty minutes. It was up to Ronaldo to save the day for his team. He had scored their only goal and every time he got the ball, the Germans tried their best to foul him. They knew what a dangerous opponent he was.

In the last minute of the first half, Ronaldo was a blur of movement once more. Just outside the penalty area, he turned quickly, faked to shoot and shifted the ball to the right. The next thing the goalkeeper knew, it was in the top corner of his net.

Goooooooooooooooooooooaaaaaaaaaaaaaaaaaalllllllllllll llllllllllllllll!!!!!!!!!!!!!!!!!!!!!

Ronaldo didn't even look surprised or excited by his wonder-strike. He just jogged calmly back to the centre circle for kick-off. Fifteen minutes later, he completed his first European hat-trick.

'This is amazing!' the TV commentator shouted. 'It's Ronaldo vs Bayer Leverkusen and it's now 4–3!'

It was still a week until Ronaldo's eighteenth birthday, and yet he was playing against experienced defenders and making them look like fools. How were you meant to stop him? Ronaldo was too quick, too skilful and too powerful. What a lethal combination! Behind that skinny frame was a beast.

Against Utrecht, Ronaldo shrugged off the big centre-back's tackles once, then twice, before smashing the ball into the net. 1–0! Twenty minutes later, he shrugged off the other centre-back and dribbled around the keeper. 2–0! Just before full-time, he made it 3–0 and hat-trick number two. The Utrecht defence lay sprawled across the grass, exhausted and defeated.

Ronaldo finished his first season in Dutch football with an amazing thirty-five goals in thirty-six games. It was a total that made Romário look like an average striker.

'The defences must have got easier since I left!' his Brazilian teammate joked with him.

In the 1995–96 season, Ronaldo picked up exactly where he had left off. In the Dutch League, he scored two against Heerenveen, then three against De Graafschap. In the UEFA Cup, he scored five in a single game against MyPa from Finland.

Just when it looked like Ronaldo might beat his previous scoring record, though, he suffered a setback. By Christmas, both of his knees were swollen and painful. He was struggling to walk, let alone run.

'It's pretty normal for a teenager like you,' the PSV doctor explained. 'You're still growing, and you've played a lot of football. That puts a lot of strain on your body. Rest for a few weeks, and see how it feels.'

Ronaldo thanked the doctor but there was one thing he was particularly worried about. 'Do you think this will affect my pace?' he asked as he left. As a striker, that was his most dangerous weapon.

The doctor gave his most reassuring smile. 'With

the right care and attention, you'll be as fast as ever!'

After a few weeks of rest, however, Ronaldo's knees didn't feel any better. He was desperate to return to the pitch as soon as possible. Football was his life and it had all been going so well…

Ronaldo didn't want to sit and wait for his injury to improve. He decided to have an operation and then return to Brazil to work hard on his recovery. Romário recommended a physio called Filé who had helped him with his knee problems.

Ronaldo missed PSV's UEFA Cup quarter-final defeat to Barcelona, but he returned just in time for the Dutch Cup Final against Sparta Rotterdam. It was a great chance for him to win his first trophy in European football.

When Ronaldo came on in the second-half, PSV were already 3–1 up. He didn't score but he did set up his team's fourth goal.

'We've won it!' Ronaldo cheered loudly. It felt really good to be back.

The big silver trophy was passed along the stage, from player to player. Ronaldo was one of the last in

the line, but the PSV fans had saved a special cheer
for him. With his shirt collar up and his earrings
sparkling, he looked like the next football superstar.
But the big grin on his face showed that he was still
just a kid who loved playing the beautiful game.

CHAPTER 10

OLYMPIC GOALS

Two years after the 1994 World Cup, Ronaldo returned to the USA to play for Brazil again, in the summer Olympic Games. This time, he was one of his country's stars and there was a gold medal up for grabs.

'Let's do this!' he told Rivaldo happily as they landed in baking hot Miami.

Brazil had never won the Olympic football tournament before. They had won silver medals in 1984 and 1988, but never gold. It was a fantastic opportunity for Ronaldo and his teammates to make history and show once again that 'The Beautiful Game' belonged to Brazil.

The squad was very strong. Bebeto and Aldair were the senior stars leading the nation's next talented generation. Powerful left-back Roberto Carlos played for Inter Milan in Italy and little playmaker Juninho played for Middlesbrough in England. Then there were the 'Two Rs' – Ronaldo and Rivaldo.

The squad was so strong, in fact, that Ronaldo started on the bench in the first match against Japan. He even had to change the name on the back of his shirt to 'Ronaldinho' ('Little Ronaldo') because there was an older 'Ronaldo', Ronaldo Guiaro, playing i n defence.

Despite all their amazing talent, Brazil got off to an awful start. As Ronaldo ran onto the field after sixty minutes, they were losing 1–0.

'Go change the game!' Roberto Carlos urged him as they high-fived.

Ronaldo did change the game, but he didn't change the scoreline. Every time he dropped deep to get the ball, there were three or four Japanese players surrounding him. Ronaldo tried to take on the whole team, twisting and turning, shifting his body from side to side. Sadly, he couldn't quite beat them all. He was a superstar, not a superhero.

Some of his teammates were very disappointed after the defeat, but not Ronaldo. 'Don't worry, I'm just getting started!' he assured them.

Ronaldo started the next match against Hungary and scored the opening goal. A long ball bounced over the centre-back's head and Ronaldo was onto it in a flash. He dribbled into the penalty area, round the goalkeeper, and tapped the ball into the empty net.

Goooooooooooooooooooooaaaaaaaaaaaaaaaaalllllllllllll llllllllllllllll!!!!!!!!!!!!!!!!!!!!!

Ronaldo ran towards the corner flag with his arms out wide like an aeroplane. 'Come on!' he screamed, telling his teammates to follow him. The stand behind the goal was a blur of yellow flags and shirts. The Brazilian party was under way.

Against Nigeria, there were defenders everywhere, blocking the route to goal. Who had the special skills to score? Ronaldo! He nutmegged Sunday Oliseh with ease. Oliseh tried to hold him back but that was a mistake. No-one could hold Ronaldo back. He broke free and thumped the ball into the bottom corner. 1–0!

Goooooooooooooooooooooaaaaaaaaaaaaaaaaaallllllllllll llllllllllllllll!!!!!!!!!!!!!!!!!!!!!

Ronaldo's face lit up and he punched the air with his fists. Thanks to him, Brazil were going through to the next round.

'What would we do without you?' Rivaldo said with a smile as they hugged near the halfway line.

They were feeling confident, perhaps a little too confident. In the quarter-final, Ghana took advantage and took a 2–1 lead.

'What's going on?' Brazil's goalkeeper Dida shouted at his teammates. 'Wake up!'

Suddenly, Ronaldo came to life. Juninho spotted his run and took a quick free kick. Ronaldo struck a first-time shot. 2–2!

After watching and waiting at the World Cup, it felt amazing to Ronaldo to be the national hero now. He jumped up into Aldair's arms.

'Go get another goal!' the defender ordered.

Ronaldo raced after Bebeto's brilliant pass. A defender slid in for the tackle, but Ronaldo got there first. He was on the left side of the six-yard box and the angle was getting tighter and tighter. It looked impossible to score. But as the goalkeeper dived at his feet, Ronaldo chipped the ball over him and it curled into the far corner. 3–2!

'You're a genius!' Bebeto cried out as Ronaldo lifted him up into the air.

Surely, Brazil would now go all the way and claim the Olympic Gold?

In the semi-finals, they faced Nigeria again. At half-time, it was 3–1 to Brazil. It looked like the Seleção were cruising to the final. When Ronaldo was substituted after eighty-five minutes, they were still winning 3–2. They just needed to defend well and keep things tight.

But without their superstar, the team of Brazil collapsed. Nigeria's Nwankwo Kanu scrambled the ball into the net. 3–3! Then in extra time, Kanu broke Brazilian hearts by scoring again. It was the golden goal.

Watching from the bench, Ronaldo couldn't believe his eyes. What a disaster!

'How did we let that happen?' he asked in the dressing room, but the only response was silence. They had let their country down.

'We have one last chance to make things right,' the manager Mário Zagallo reminded his players. 'We can't win the Gold Medal or the Silver, but we can take home the Bronze. Let's make sure of that!'

Brazil were so determined that their opponents Portugal had no chance. As Juninho dribbled infield, Ronaldo made a storming run through the middle. When the pass arrived, he unleashed all of his frustration on the ball. 1–0!

After that, Brazil brought out their most beautiful game. Pass, pass, skill, goal! Pass, pass, skill, goal! 2–0, 3–0, 4–0, 5–0! The fans in the stadium loved to see their team playing such entertaining football.

At the final whistle, the players hugged each other. They hadn't won the medal that they wanted but Bronze was definitely better than nothing.

Ronaldo was particularly pleased with his own

performances. With five goals, he had lived up to his reputation as 'the next big thing'. He had shown the world what he could do, and he was still only nineteen years old.

The top clubs in Europe were queuing up to sign Ronaldo. Where would he be playing next season? Inter Milan? Barcelona? He wasn't sure, but he knew that it wouldn't be PSV. Ronaldo had enjoyed his time in the Netherlands, but it was time to move on to bigger and better things.

CHAPTER 11

BARCELONA

In the end, Inter Milan decided not to sign Ronaldo because they were worried about his injuries. So, Ronaldo followed in his friend Romário's footsteps and joined Barcelona instead. The Spanish club were so excited about signing Ronaldo that they agreed to break the world transfer record. It was a big risk: £13.2 million for a nineteen-year-old striker with knee problems.

There was lots of pressure on Ronaldo, especially now that he was the most expensive footballer ever. To make life even harder for himself, he took the Number 9 shirt at Barcelona. That was the shirt worn by club legends like César Rodríguez, László

Kubala, and even Johan Cruyff. Was it a good idea to get the fans so excited straight away?

'Why not? I scored lots of goals at PSV,' Ronaldo told his new Brazilian teammate, Giovanni. 'Now, I'm ready for the big time!'

Barcelona centre-back Fernando Couto decided to make sure. In training, it was Fernando vs Ronaldo, the new defender against the new attacker. Who would win?

When Luís Figo played the ball into Ronaldo's path, Fernando thought he could deal with the danger. He was a skinny kid, after all, with his back to goal. If he marked his opponent tightly, how could he escape? With a nutmeg! In a flash, Ronaldo flicked the ball through Fernando's legs and burst into the box. He was so fast that no-one could catch up with him.

The other players had stopped to watch the amazing show of skill. Ronaldo just had Vítor left to beat. He faked to shoot one way but as the keeper dived at his feet, he turned the other way. Ronaldo's finale was a pass into the empty goal.

'Okay,' Fernando admitted to Luís afterwards. 'He's ready!'

Ronaldo made his Barcelona debut in the 1996 Spanish Super Cup Final against Atlético Madrid. As he ran out onto the pitch, he looked so calm but, on the inside, he was feeling a little nervous. Well, as nervous as Ronaldo ever felt about football, his favourite thing in the world.

When he got the ball, Ronaldo only had one thing on his mind – attack. He dribbled through three defenders as if they were the fruit trees back in Bento Ribeiro. From outside the penalty area, he fired a low shot into the bottom corner.

Gooooooooooooooooooooaaaaaaaaaaaaaaaaalllllllllllll lllllllllllll!!!!!!!!!!!!!!!!!!!!

With a big grin on his face, Ronaldo stretched out his arms for his trademark celebration. Wherever he went, he made scoring great goals look so easy.

'Five minutes – that's how long it took you to get used to Spanish football!' Giovanni joked, giving him a big hug.

The Barcelona fans rubbed their hands with glee.

Their new striker was even better than they had expected.

In the last minute, Giovanni ran through the Atlético defence and set up Ronaldo for his second debut goal. The whole team celebrated a huge 5–2 victory.

'We're going to have a lot of fun together this season!' Luís said with a smile.

There was just no stopping Ronaldo. When he won the ball on the halfway line, the Compostela defenders kicked his ankles and pulled his shirt but that only spurred him on. He was like a magnet, drawn towards the goal. Ronaldo escaped and dribbled towards the penalty area at top speed. As he entered the box, he moved the ball from one foot to the other to beat another two defenders.

'Shoot! Shoot!' the fans shouted. What a wondergoal it would be.

Ronaldo was losing his balance, but he still managed to hook the ball into the net.

Goooooooooooooooooooooaaaaaaaaaaaaaaaalllllllllllll llllllllllllll!!!!!!!!!!!!!!!!!!!

It was Ronaldo's favourite kind of goal, the kind of goal that he had perfected during his early street football days. The only defender that he hadn't dribbled past was the goalkeeper.

'Next time, I'll go around him too!' he promised himself.

On the bench, the Barcelona manager Bobby Robson had his hands on his head in shock. He couldn't believe what he had just seen, and neither could the Spanish newspapers.

'Pelé Returns!' was the headline the next day.

Ronaldo was delighted with all of his goals but what he really wanted was trophies. That's what made a talented player world-class. Real Madrid ran away with the Spanish League, but Barcelona made it to the Cup Winners' Cup Final against PSG.

It was Ronaldo and Giovanni against their international teammates Raí and Leonardo. Who would win the battle of Brazil's best players?

Barcelona started brightly. Luís passed to Ronaldo, who passed back for the one-two. Luís's shot drifted just wide of the post.

'Unlucky, mate!' Ronaldo clapped. He loved to play exciting, attacking football.

Just before half-time, Ronaldo got the ball on the left side of the penalty area. His first touch was heavy and so Bruno N'Gotty slid in for the tackle. What a mistake! He had forgotten about Ronaldo's speed. He got to the ball first and tripped over N'Gotty's legs. Penalty!

Ronaldo picked up the ball and placed it on the spot. The cup final pressure didn't bother him. His run-up was long but slow. By the time he kicked the ball, the goalkeeper had already dived to his right. Ronaldo calmly placed his penalty in the opposite corner.

Gooooooooooooooooooooaaaaaaaaaaaaaaaaaalllllllllllll llllllllllllllll!!!!!!!!!!!!!!!!!!!!

'Cool as you like!' Luis Enrique cheered, jumping on Ronaldo's back.

That goal turned out to be the matchwinner, and the cupwinner. At the final whistle, Ronaldo walked over to the Barca fans and threw his arms up in the air. They roared back in delight.

Robson ran over to hug his hero. 'Thank you, you've made a great team even better!' he shouted.

As the captain, Gheorghe Popescu, lifted the trophy above his head, Ronaldo jumped up and down with his teammates. What a way to end his incredible first season in Spain. Ronaldo had a top European trophy to go with his FIFA World Player of the Year award and a club record total of forty-seven goals. No Barcelona player had ever scored so many in a single season.

'He's just amazing,' Ronaldo's teammate Luís told the media. 'He was born with a special football talent.'

CHAPTER 12

INTER MILAN

Sadly, the 1996–97 season was Ronaldo's only season at Barcelona. In Summer 1997, he was on the move again. Italian giants Inter Milan had changed their mind about his knee problems. Suddenly, they were willing to take the risk and pay a lot of money.

The Barcelona club president Josep Lluís Núñez did his best to keep Ronaldo at the club but Inter refused to give up. In the end, their president Massimo Moratti handed over a cheque for £25 million. That meant that Ronaldo was the most expensive player in the world again.

When he arrived in Milan, big crowds filled the central square to greet him. The fans hoped that their new Brazilian Number 10 could shoot them all the way to their first Serie A title in ten years. Ronaldo joined a very international attack featuring Frenchman Youri Djorkaeff, Chilean Iván Zamorano and Nigerian Nwankwo Kanu.

'Hey, don't even mention the Olympics!' he joked with Nwankwo.

There were two reasons why this was Ronaldo's greatest challenge yet. The first was that the Italian League was very competitive. Inter's biggest rivals were Juventus and AC Milan but there were lots of other good teams too, like Lazio, Parma and Roma.

The second was that Italy was famous for having the best defences in the world. Lazio had Alessandro Nesta, Juventus had Ciro Ferrara, while AC Milan had Paolo Maldini *and* Marcel Desailly. Not only were the defenders big and tough, but they were also clever and quick. If Ronaldo really wanted to test himself as a striker, he was in the right place.

This time, Ronaldo didn't score on his league debut. He played well but every time he went to shoot, the defenders blocked it or caught him offside.

It was substitute Álvaro Recoba who came to the rescue for Inter. At the end, it was Álvaro who the players hugged, and it was Álvaro's name that the fans sang.

'Next time,' Ronaldo told himself. Even the best defences in the world couldn't keep him quiet for long. He was born to score.

Against Bologna, Youri passed the ball to Ronaldo on the edge of the area. There was a defender right in front of him but this time, Ronaldo was thinking one step ahead. In a flash, he fooled the defender and fired a left-foot shot into the bottom corner.

Goooooooooooooooooooooaaaaaaaaaaaaaaaaaallllllllllll llllllllllllll!!!!!!!!!!!!!!!!!!

Ronaldo punched the air. He was off the mark in Italy!

After that, the goals flew in, game after game. Ronaldo scored against Fiorentina, Lazio, Parma, and best of all, against AC in the big Milan derby.

And even when he wasn't scoring, Ronaldo was still Inter's leader. His teammates relied on him to be the matchwinner and he hardly ever let them down. In a crunch game against their title rivals Juventus, Ronaldo shrugged off Paulo Montero, escaped from Moreno Torricelli's lunge, and then delivered a perfect cross for Youri to slide in at the back post. 1–0!

It was a moment of magic to celebrate Ronaldo's latest award, the Ballon d'Or. He was the best player in the world and he wanted everyone to know it.

Moratti was delighted with his superstar signing. The risk had been worth it. Ronaldo was the top scorer in Serie A and Inter were top of the table.

'You're a genius!' the club president cheered, hugging his favourite Brazilian striker.

Ronaldo was enjoying himself in Italy. At twenty years old, he was still improving his game, adding to that amazing natural talent. He was learning lots from playing against the best defences in the world.

Ronaldo had a lot of responsibility at Inter but he didn't mind. Besides, the team wasn't all about him. There were excellent defenders like Javier Zanetti and Giuseppe Bergomi, and brilliant midfielders like

Youri and Diego Simeone. Together, they had their
eyes on the prize – the Serie A title.

Ronaldo's goals powered Inter towards glory. No-
one could stop him scoring; not Atalanta, not AC
Milan, not Sampdoria, not Roma and not Udinese.

But what about Juventus? The whole season
rested on Juventus vs Inter Milan at the Stadio delle
Alpi. It was always the most difficult away trip of the
season because the atmosphere was so intense.

'We need something *really* special from you
tonight,' his manager Luigi Simoni told Ronaldo
before kick-off.

'I'll do my best,' he replied with a friendly,
confident smile.

In the first half, however, Ronaldo hardly touched
the ball. The Juventus defenders followed him
everywhere and the Juventus midfielders Edgar
Davids and Zinedine Zidane made sure that passes
didn't reach him.

After twenty minutes, Alessandro Del Piero
dribbled into the Inter penalty area and scored. 1–0!

Ronaldo kicked at the grass in frustration. He was

angry, and it was never a good idea to make him angry. 'Come on!' he shouted to his teammates.

As Ronaldo got the ball and tried to turn, two Juventus players fouled him at the same time. He fell to the floor in agony.

'Ref!' Diego protested. 'They're doing it every time!'

Ronaldo got up and took the free kick himself. He was determined to show Juventus that they couldn't stop him like that. His powerful, curling shot flew just over the crossbar.

'So close!' Youri cried out next to him.

'Don't worry, I'll score eventually,' Ronaldo promised.

With twenty minutes to go, he battled for the ball and won it in the Juventus penalty area. Ronaldo could see Montero rushing towards him, so he cleverly poked the ball around him. As he tried to run on to it, the defender barged him to the ground.

'Penalty!' the Inter players screamed but the referee shook his head.

Ronaldo couldn't believe it. It was a blatant foul at a crucial moment.

'Why didn't you point to the spot?' he asked the referee furiously. 'I was about to score, and he ran into me on purpose!'

It just wasn't Ronaldo's day. In the final minute of the match, the ball bounced up in front of him in the box. One last chance! For once, he panicked and swung his leg wildly at it. The ball soared high into the stands.

Ronaldo stood there, staring down at the grass below his feet. Inter's big title dream was over.

Thankfully, that wasn't the only trophy that they were challenging for. They were also into the UEFA Cup Final against their Italian rivals Lazio.

'This is a big night for you,' Youri told Ronaldo on the pitch in Paris. 'Lead us to victory!'

Iván and Javier got the first two goals, but Ronaldo was always Inter's danger man. Again and again, he tormented the Lazio defence with his speed and skill. Every time he got the ball, the excitement grew around the stadium. Could Ronaldo cap off an exceptional performance with another big cup final goal?

When Benoît Cauet played the through-ball, the Lazio defenders appealed for offside. But no, Ronaldo had timed his run perfectly and now he was through on goal. As the goalkeeper raced out to the edge of his area, Ronaldo thought about shooting but that wasn't his style. Instead, he went for the stepover, dribbled round the keeper and then passed the ball into the empty net.

Goooooooooooooooooooaaaaaaaaaaaaaaaallllllllllll llllllllllllllll!!!!!!!!!!!!!!!!!!!

What a way to seal the victory! At the final whistle, Ronaldo pumped his fists and roared up at the sky. It was trophy time for him and his Inter teammates. With a Brazilian flag wrapped around his waist and a crowd of photographers around him, Ronaldo lifted the UEFA Cup high above his head. He couldn't get enough of that winning feeling.

CHAPTER 13

WORLD CUP 1998

That summer, Ronaldo had the chance to carry on the winning feeling at the 1998 World Cup. He had been looking forward to the tournament ever since the 1994 final in the USA. Yes, he already had one winners' medal, but he wanted to earn it properly this time. He wanted to become Brazil's national hero.

There was no question that Ronaldo was now his country's best striker. He had the Number 9 shirt to prove it. He had scored fifteen goals in 1997 alone, as Brazil won the Copa América in style. In the final against Bolivia, he had hit a left-foot rocket into the top corner.

Gooooooooooooooooooooaaaaaaaaaaaaaaaalllllllllllll llllllllllllll!!!!!!!!!!!!!!!!!!!!!

Brazil were the Champions of South America, but could they become Champions of the World again? As the squad travelled to France, Ronaldo was feeling as confident as ever. Romário was no longer part of the team but his friends Roberto Carlos, Rivaldo and Giovanni were. Together, they were the next generation of Brazilian talent.

'It's our time to shine!' Ronaldo said, his eyes wide with excitement.

The manager Mário Zagallo wanted Brazil to play 'The Beautiful Game' again. For their first group match, against Scotland, he picked Ronaldo, Rivaldo, Giovanni and Bebeto all in the same team.

'Looks like I'm going to have a lot of defending to do!' Roberto Carlos grumbled. He preferred to attack, but so did every Brazilian.

They took the lead after only five minutes against Scotland, but it wasn't Ronaldo who scored, or Rivaldo. In fact, it wasn't any of Brazil's fearsome four. It was their defensive midfielder César Sampaio.

'That's meant to be your job!' Roberto Carlos joked with Ronaldo as the whole team celebrated together in front of a sea of yellow.

At half-time, however, the score was 1–1. Despite all of their attacking talent, Brazil were struggling to score against the Scottish defence. Eventually, they won the game but only thanks to a fluky own goal after a brilliant run from their right-back, Cafu.

At the final whistle, there was great relief amongst the Brazil players. But as Ronaldo walked off the pitch with Rivaldo and Bebeto, he wasn't satisfied. 'We've got work to do,' he told them.

In the next match against Morocco, they were like a totally different strikeforce. As the ball fell to Rivaldo, Ronaldo was already on the move. The pass was perfect, so good that Ronaldo didn't even need to take a touch. On the edge of the penalty area, he struck the shot on the half-volley. The ball dipped down into the bottom corner.

Gooooooooooooooooooooaaaaaaaaaaaaaaaaalllllllllllll llllllllllllll!!!!!!!!!!!!!!!!!!

Ronaldo finally had his first World Cup goal! Joy

and relief rushed through his body as he raced over to his teammates on the touchline. It was a moment that he wanted to share with everyone. The whole squad hugged their hero.

Brazil had found their best attacking football.

Cafu crossed for Rivaldo. 2–0!

Ronaldo dribbled through the Morocco defence and passed to Bebeto. 3–0!

A Mexican wave spread around the stadium in Nantes. There was plenty for the fans to cheer about. Brazil's front three had scored a goal each.

'That's more like it, guys!' Roberto Carlos cheered.

Brazil finished top of Group A, even after a 2–1 defeat to Norway. Their stars were saving their energy for Round Two. They were up against their South American rivals, Chile, and Ronaldo was up against his Inter Milan teammate, Iván Zamorano.

'Good luck!' they said to each other before the big kick-off.

In a brilliant first half, Brazil stormed into a 3–0 lead. They weren't classic wondergoals, however, full of tricks and flair. The first was a header, the

95

second was a scramble in the box, and the third was a penalty. They weren't winning in style, but they were winning. That was the most important thing.

'Now we can bring out all our tricks!' Ronaldo shouted happily.

Denílson passed to César, who passed to Rivaldo, who flicked it through to Denílson.

Olé!

This was the entertaining football that the Brazil fans had been waiting for. Denílson slipped the ball across to Ronaldo, who dribbled forward. He lifted the ball cheekily over the goalkeeper's diving body.

Gooooooooooooooooooaaaaaaaaaaaaaaaalllllllllllll lllllllllllll!!!!!!!!!!!!!!!!!!!

Ronaldo ran straight over to Denílson. 'That's samba football, right there!'

Brazil expected more of the same against Denmark in the quarter-final, but they were in for a bit of a shock. After two minutes, they were 1–0 down. Their supporters fell silent but fortunately, their players didn't panic. Why would they, when they had so many amazing attackers on the pitch?

Ronaldo dropped deeper to get the ball. Once he got it, he turned and played a defence-splitting pass to Bebeto. 1–1!

Fifteen minutes later, Ronaldo did it again, but this time he set up Rivaldo to score – 2–1!

'Thanks, mate!' Rivaldo said as they hugged by the corner flag. The supporters had found their voices again and they danced in their seats.

The match finished 3–2 and Brazil were through to another World Cup semi-final. Ronaldo was pleased with his assists but, as always, he wanted to score more goals. That's what he was there for as his nation's Number 9. That's what he was born to do.

The Number 9 for the Netherlands was Patrick Kluivert. Kluivert played for Ajax and he had been Ronaldo's rival during his days at PSV. They were the same age and two of the best strikers in the world. Ronaldo was *the* best, however, and he wasn't going to let anyone take his crown.

At half-time, it was Ronaldo 0 Kluivert 0, and Brazil 0 Netherlands 0. Just after the break, Roberto Carlos passed to Rivaldo, who had the space and time to look up. He spotted Ronaldo on the move again and delivered the pass on a plate. Ronaldo's first touch was fantastic and his second was a shot that nutmegged the keeper.

Goooooooooooooooooooaaaaaaaaaaaaaaaaallllllllllll llllllllllllll!!!!!!!!!!!!!!!!!!

It was 1–0 to Ronaldo and Brazil! How should he celebrate his crucial strike? He started running towards his teammates but then stopped still. 'Let them come to me,' he thought to himself. '*I'm* the hero!'

They looked like they were cruising into the final but late on, Kluivert jumped up and headed the ball home. 1–1!

'No!' Ronaldo groaned. He had one last opportunity to win the game, but a Dutch defender cleared his bicycle kick off the line.

The match went to extra time and after extra time, the match went to penalties. The atmosphere in the stadium grew tenser and tenser. Even Brazil's joyful fans were feeling a little nervous.

Ronaldo sat down on the grass and stretched out his tired legs.

'How are you feeling?' his goalkeeper, Taffarel, asked.

'Ready,' Ronaldo replied without even thinking. His usual smile was gone, replaced by a focused look.

Ronaldo went first for his country. With the pressure on, he made no mistake. The back of the net bulged. Advantage to Brazil!

Ronaldo punched the air as he jogged back to the halfway line. Winning another World Cup meant so much to him.

When Taffarel saved Ronald de Boer's spot-kick, Ronaldo and his teammates raced to celebrate with their goalkeeper.

'We're in the final!' they chanted together.

CHAPTER 14

A FINAL TO FORGET

During the 1998 World Cup, Ronaldo shared a
room with his friend and teammate, Roberto Carlos.
They had known each other for years and they had
lots of things in common – laughing, partying and,
of course, playing football.

However, on the day of the final, they were
feeling very different emotions. After lunch,
Ronaldo was quiet and decided to take a nap.
Roberto Carlos was way too excited to sleep. Before
every big match, there were so many thoughts
going through his head and so much adrenaline
buzzing through his body.

To try to calm himself down, Roberto Carlos

decided to listen to music. He plugged in his headphones, so that he didn't wake up his roommate. Ronaldo needed as much rest as possible ahead of the biggest match of his life. There was so much pressure resting on his young shoulders, the weight of the whole Brazilian nation.

Half an hour later, Roberto Carlos heard strange sounds in the room. At first, he thought it was part of the song but when he took off his headphones, he realised that the sounds were actually coming from the bed next to him. Ronaldo was shaking and struggling to breathe.

Roberto Carlos rushed over to his friend. Was he just having a bad nightmare, or was it something more serious? He couldn't just stand by and hope for the best. He had to do something.

'Help!' Roberto Carlos screamed out.

Edmundo was staying in the hotel room next door. When he rushed in and saw Ronaldo, his jaw dropped. It didn't look good at all. 'What's going on?' he asked.

'I don't know!' Roberto Carlos replied tearfully.

He was so worried about his friend.

César was the next to arrive and he managed to open his teammate's mouth. 'Breathe!' he kept shouting. After a few minutes, Ronaldo stopped shaking and fell into a deep sleep.

Soon, most of the Brazil players were there in the room, looking panicked and confused. What had happened to their star? When the team doctor, Lídio Toledo, arrived on the scene, he told everyone to leave.

'Out!' he ordered. 'He needs space and so do I. Let me do my job.'

When Ronaldo woke up a few hours later, he said that he felt fine. Toledo took him to the hospital for medical tests, but they couldn't find anything wrong with him. It was a total mystery.

Meanwhile, the rest of the squad travelled to the Stade de France in stunned silence. Their usual samba spirit was gone. They were missing their leader. Could they win the World Cup without him?

With three hours to go before kick-off, the Brazil

coaches didn't know what to do. Was Ronaldo really well enough to play in the final?

'Please let me play!' Ronaldo begged his manager Mário Zagallo. 'I can't miss this match – you need me! I'm going out on that pitch no matter what.'

Zagallo had already announced his starting line-up, with Edmundo up front and Ronaldo on the bench. Meanwhile, 160 million football-mad Brazilians were furious. Why wasn't their superstar striker in the team? 'Ronaldo *has* to play!' they argued.

Everyone knew that Ronaldo was a big game player. The 1997 Cup Winner's Cup, the 1997 Copa América and the 1998 UEFA Cup – not only had he won all three competitions, but he had also scored in all three finals. The nation believed that he would do the same in the 1998 World Cup Final.

Was there still time for Zagallo to change his mind? Yes. Suddenly, Ronaldo was back in Brazil's starting line-up.

'Are you sure you're okay?' Leonardo asked Ronaldo in the tunnel.

Ronaldo nodded but he was the last player to walk out onto the pitch in Paris. He didn't look his usual happy self, and neither did any of his teammates. After such an upsetting day, they weren't ready to play in a World Cup Final.

Ronaldo did his best for his country. He got the ball and dribbled at France's right-back, Lilian Thuram. After a couple of stepovers, he crossed towards Bebeto, but the goalkeeper caught it.

'Well played!' the Brazilian supporters applauded loudly. It was a promising start from their hero.

Ronaldo's energy didn't last very long, though. His touch got heavier and heavier, and his running got slower and slower. Soon, he wasn't having any impact on the game at all. Ronaldo was a shadow of the usual striker. Something was clearly wrong.

'Stay focused!' captain Dunga shouted to his players but it was no use. Brazil were in a daze and they had no chance against fired-up France.

With the home crowd roaring them on, Zinedine Zidane scored two headers in the first half. Ronaldo could only stand and watch as his World Cup dream disappeared before his eyes.

When he collided with the France goalkeeper Fabian Barthez, the other Brazilian players froze in fear. Cafu raced over to check on his teammate.

'What's wrong?' he asked.

Ronaldo winced. 'Don't worry, his knee caught me in the side. I'm fine.'

Despite his health problems earlier that day, he carried on and played the full ninety minutes. Every time Zagallo thought about taking him off, Ronaldo said he wanted to keep playing. At the final whistle, he stood alone, staring down at the pitch, thinking what might have been. If he was fully fit, would Ronaldo have won the final for Brazil? He would never know the answer to that question.

'I'm sorry,' Youri, his Inter Milan teammate said, giving him a hug.

'I'm sorry too,' Ronaldo thought to himself. He was sorry for Brazil – the fans and the players. He felt like he had let them all down when it mattered most. Perhaps they would have been better off without him in the World Cup Final.

'Come on, we've still got 2002 *and* 2006!' Roberto Carlos said, trying to cheer Ronaldo up. He was just happy that his friend was feeling better. It was a final to forget for the whole of Brazil.

CHAPTER 15

SIDELINED

Ronaldo couldn't wait to put his World Cup woe behind him. He returned to Italy and focused on winning the Serie A title with Inter Milan. Another top trophy would make everything better.

Ronaldo's 1998–99 season started with a penalty against Piacenza. One game, one goal – he was delighted to get off the mark straight away.

'Nice strike!' Roberto Baggio cheered.

The Inter fans were excited about their new star strikeforce. 'Ronie and Roby' they called them. Together, they combined skill and scoring. Juventus and AC Milan would have to watch out.

However, behind the scenes, the picture wasn't

quite so positive. Ronaldo's old knee problems had come back to haunt him. At the World Cup, the Brazil doctors had given him injections to relieve the pain and allow him to keep playing. Now that he was back at Inter, the pain was getting worse.

There was no way that Ronaldo could play every game of a long, hard season. The manager Luigi Simoni had to pick which matches were more important – the Champions League or the Italian League? He chose the Champions League.

Ronaldo couldn't wait to play in Europe's top competition. He had won the Cup Winners' Cup in 1997, then the UEFA Cup in 1998. Could he complete the hat-trick by winning the Champions League in 1999?

With such high expectations, Ronaldo only scored one goal in six European games. He still showed flashes of his old brilliance, but that explosive speed was gone.

'I can't burst into the box like I used to,' he admitted to the Inter physio.

It was so frustrating, especially as Ronaldo was

still only twenty-two years old. He was meant to be approaching his footballing prime.

It turned into a disastrous season for Inter Milan. By April, they were out of the Champions League and only eighth position in Serie A. The only positive was Ronaldo's return to form. A month's rest had made all the difference. Wearing the captain's armband, he finally felt like his old self again.

Against Roma, Ronaldo made a powerful run through the middle. It felt so good to race past defenders once more. With the fans cheering loudly, he collected Roberto's pass, dribbled round the goalkeeper and scored.

Goooooooooooooooooooooaaaaaaaaaaaaaaaaalllllllllllllll llllllllllllll!!!!!!!!!!!!!!!!!!!!!

Ronaldo ran towards the fans with a huge grin on his face. It was the kind of goal that he used to score week in, week out.

'You're back to your best!' Iván cheered.

In the second half, the Chilean set up a second goal for Ronaldo. 'I'm just building up your confidence again!' he teased.

It was working. The Brazilian scored in his next three matches in a row. 'Why does the season have to end now?' Ronaldo moaned to Youri. 'I feel like I'm just getting started!'

'Hey, there's always next season,' his teammate replied.

For the 1999–2000 season, Inter Milan signed Christian Vieri to play up front with Ronaldo, Roberto and Iván. On paper, they now had the best strikeforce in the world. The Serie A title, the Champions League – there was no limit to what they could achieve, just as long as Ronaldo could stay fit.

Against Lecce in November 1999, Inter were 5–0 up after fifty minutes. Ronaldo was feeling good after scoring another goal. But as he ran in to beat a defender to the ball, he felt his right knee twist awkwardly.

'Argghhhhhh!' he cried out in pain.

Ronaldo played the pass and then hobbled over to the touchline. He really wanted to carry on playing, but the club physios wouldn't let him.

'We're already 5–0 up!' his new manager Marcello

Lippi told him. He was desperate to protect his superstar. 'There's absolutely no point in you making the injury worse.'

For a minute, Ronaldo stood by the dugout, testing his knee. Eventually, however, he accepted his manager's decision. He took Álvaro Recoba's coat and sat down grumpily on the bench. Ronaldo hated missing even a few moments of football. Every second on the pitch was a chance to score.

Unfortunately, Ronaldo's injury turned out to be a lot more serious than anyone expected. He had ruptured a tendon in his knee.

'What does that mean?' he asked. 'A few weeks out?'

The club doctor shook his head and frowned. 'I'm afraid there's a lot of damage,' he explained. 'You're going to need an operation. If all goes well, you could be back in four months.'

'Four months?' Ronaldo exploded in shock. 'If all goes well?'

It was the worst news possible but arguing wouldn't help the terrible situation. His next question was calm and sensible. 'So, how soon can I have the operation?'

After the surgery, Ronaldo worked hard on his recovery. In between boring gym sessions, he tried to stay busy and take his mind off football. He returned to Brazil and married his girlfriend Milene Domingues. Not only that, but they also got ready to have their first child together.

'Life is good!' Ronaldo told his wedding guests in Rio de Janeiro. 'I have a wonderful wife, I'll soon be a father, and I'll soon be back on the football pitch too!'

In the end, Ronaldo's big Inter comeback arrived just days after the birth of his son, Ronald. The doctors decided that he was fit enough to play the last thirty minutes of the Coppa Italia Final against Lazio. Six long months had passed since the nightmare at Lecce. It felt like a lifetime. Ronaldo just wanted to get back to doing what he did best – playing football.

Early in the second half, Lazio were winning 2–1. Lippi turned to speak to his star striker, his super sub.

'Are you ready?' he asked.

Ronaldo nodded eagerly.

'Good, get warmed up!'

As Ronaldo ran onto the field, the atmosphere in the Stadio Olimpico grew even tenser. The world's best player was back. The Lazio fans were scared, and the Inter fans were hopeful. They needed a hero to come to the rescue.

Ronaldo was up against his old Barcelona teammate, Fernando Couto. Their battle began. Iván flicked the ball on and Ronaldo was off, dribbling towards Fernando. On the edge of the penalty area, he went for one of his trademark stepovers. But as his right leg landed, there was a loud SNAP!

Unbearable pain shot through Ronaldo's knee. He tumbled to the floor, screaming. The whole stadium fell silent. It was a tragedy for the whole footballing world. Ronaldo had only been on the pitch for seven minutes.

Inter teammates new and old stood together in shock. Diego Simeone now played for Lazio, but he still rushed over to check on his friend. It didn't look good at all.

'Stay strong!' Diego shouted to him.

Ronaldo left the field on a stretcher, with a hand hiding the tears streaming down his face. He was sidelined again, and this time, it wouldn't be just for six months. It would be for the entire 2000–01 season and more.

CHAPTER 16

BOUNCING BACK

2002 was meant to be Ronaldo's big year. It was meant to be the year when he would win a second World Cup for Brazil and would erase all memories of 1998's awful final defeat to France.

That was the plan but with six months to go until the start of the tournament, Ronaldo was still on the long road to recovery. He was back in the Inter Milan squad but not in the Inter Milan starting line-up. His club manager Héctor Cúper was taking things very slowly, building up Ronaldo's minutes off the bench.

'They're just trying to make sure that the Lazio disaster doesn't happen again,' Nélio Sr told his son.

Ronaldo understood that, but he didn't have time

to take things slowly. The race was on to make Brazil's World Cup squad. He hadn't played for his country for two whole years. Did the fans even remember him? Would they even want him back?

Ronaldo spoke to the national manager Luiz Felipe Scolari, whose message was clear:

'Trust me, I really want to have you there in South Korea and Japan, but first, you need to show me that you're ready. I need to know that your body can handle all that football.'

Ronaldo was determined to bounce back quickly. Away at Brescia, he finally got his chance to play from the start. He would be lining up alongside Christian Vieri in Inter's attack. It was the dream strikeforce that the fans had been waiting a long time to see.

'Let's do this!' Ronaldo said excitedly.

After eighteen minutes, he passed to Christian and then raced through to collect the one-two. As the goalkeeper rushed out, Ronaldo poked the ball straight through his legs and into the net.

Goooooooooooooooooooooaaaaaaaaaaaaaaaaalllllllllllll llllllllllllll!!!!!!!!!!!!!!!!!!!

He had missed the buzz of scoring so much. Ronaldo's smile was bigger than ever as Christian ran over to hug him.

'I'm back!' he roared.

Ten days later, Ronaldo chased after another through-ball against Verona. His pace wasn't quite so electric anymore, but he could still beat most defenders in a race. This time in the box, he had the confidence to finish in style. He faked to shoot and dribbled round the keeper before scoring. It was just like the old days again.

Goooooooooooooooooooaaaaaaaaaaaaaaaalllllllllll llllllllllllll!!!!!!!!!!!!!!!!!!!

Ronaldo jumped into Christian's arms and punched the air. He was doing exactly what Scolari had asked him to do. He was keeping his 2002 World Cup dream alive.

However, just when it looked like Ronaldo's comeback was complete, he picked up another injury. It wasn't particularly serious, but Cúper saw it as a warning sign that his striker needed to be careful.

'You've got to slow down,' he urged. 'If you push your body too hard, it will break down again.'

'I'm fine – it was just a slight thigh strain,' Ronaldo protested. 'I'm ready to play, I promise!'

The Inter manager, however, didn't listen. Ronaldo was back to playing stop-start football, and the timing was terrible. He could hear a clock ticking in his head. Scolari was watching and waiting for him to prove himself on the pitch. But instead, Ronaldo was sitting on the subs bench, miles away in Italy.

'I have to do *something!*' he told his dad. The World Cup meant everything to him.

In the end, the Brazilians hatched a cunning plan. Inter agreed to let Ronaldo return to Brazil for treatment. That was only half of the truth, however. Ronaldo was also returning to Brazil for top-secret tests. Scolari wanted to know if his star striker was ready for the World Cup.

For a whole month, Brazil's best coaches and doctors studied every aspect of Ronaldo – his speed, his movement, his mental strength, even his diet. They wanted to be absolutely sure about picking their World Cup wildcard. Finally, they reached their conclusion.

'So, is he ready?' Scolari asked nervously.

'Yes!' the team of coaches replied. 'He's as fast now as he was in 1998!'

'Yes!' the team of doctors replied. 'He's in the best shape of his life!'

Brazil's manager was delighted. His most dangerous weapon would be going to South Korea and Japan. There wasn't a defender in the world who wasn't scared of playing against Ronaldo.

'Well done!' Scolari said, patting him on the back. 'Now go back to Italy and get as much game-time, and as many goals as you can!'

Ronaldo was like a totally different player when he returned to Inter. He was faster, fitter and more fired up.

'I'm going to force my way back into Cúper's team,' he told himself, 'no matter what!'

That didn't take long at all. And as soon as he was back on the teamsheet, he was back on the scoresheet too. When a Brescia defender played a sloppy back-pass towards his keeper, Ronaldo was already on the run, and ready to pounce. His shot hit the post but bounced straight back to him. Second time lucky: 1–1!

Goooooooooooooooooooaaaaaaaaaaaaaaaalllllllllllll lllllllllllllll!!!!!!!!!!!!!!!!!!!!

'Come on!' Ronaldo screamed, shaking his fists with passion.

Three minutes later, he scored a long-range screamer – 2–1! This time, he took his shirt off and whirled it in the air. His delighted teammates tackled him to the floor and piled on top of him. Thanks to Ronaldo's goals, Inter Milan stayed top of the Serie A table with only three games to go.

Once he started, Ronaldo couldn't stop scoring. His goal against Chievo was a tap-in but his goal against Piacenza was a beauty. With his son Ronald watching in the stadium, he curled a free kick into the top corner.

Goooooooooooooooooooaaaaaaaaaaaaaaaalllllllllllll lllllllllllllll!!!!!!!!!!!!!!!!!!!!

Before the last day of the season, Inter Milan

sat one point ahead of their big rivals Juventus. Juventus travelled to Udinese, while Inter travelled to Lazio. For Ronaldo, that meant a return to the scene of his tragic injury – the Stadio Olimpico. Could he pull off the ultimate bounce-back and win the Italian League title?

Sadly, Ronaldo could not. As he trudged off the pitch with fifteen minutes to go, the scoreboard read 'LAZIO 4–2 INTER'. On the bench, Ronaldo covered his face and cried. They had got so close to glory.

The news wasn't all bad, however. No, Inter Milan didn't win the Serie A title, but with weeks to go until the 2002 World Cup, Ronaldo was finding his best form once more.

CHAPTER 17

WORLD CUP 2002: THE THREE RS

In Brazil, all anyone could talk about was 'The Three Rs'. No, it wasn't a new pop group – it was their new star football strikeforce: 09 Ronaldo, 10 Rivaldo and 11 Ronaldinho. The national team hadn't had a line-up that good since Pelé's front five in 1970.

'Hey, what about me?' Roberto Carlos asked, looking hurt. 'I'm an R too!'

'Sorry mate, your name ends with a C – Carlos,' Ronaldo explained, trying to make his friend feel better.

Ronaldo was so excited about the big tournament that he went out and got a special World Cup haircut.

'Whoa, what happened?' Ronaldinho asked, looking shocked as his teammate arrived at training. 'Did the razor break halfway through?'

It was certainly an unusual hairstyle. Ronaldo's head was completely shaved, apart from a big patch of hair at the front. He smiled. 'Hopefully now everyone will start talking about my hair and stop talking about my injuries!'

Without all the questions about his knees and thighs, Ronaldo could focus on doing his best for his country. That was worth looking silly for a few weeks.

Rivaldo curled a cross into the Turkey box. Ronaldo was the target, but it was 3 vs 1. How could he possibly score? With a clever late run, that's how! He ghosted right in between the defenders and stretched his legs out towards the ball. It bounced down into the ground and then up over the goalkeeper's arms.

Goooooooooooooooooooooaaaaaaaaaaaaaaaaalllllllllllll llllllllllllll!!!!!!!!!!!!!!!!!!!!

Ronaldo had scored for Brazil for the first time

since the 1999 Copa América. Three years! That was a very long time, especially in football and especially for a star striker like Ronaldo. A wave of emotions rushed through his brain and body – joy and relief, excitement and pride.

What a moment. Fortunately, Ronaldo had a new goal celebration for the special occasion. As he ran towards the bench, he wagged his right index finger from side to side.

'What's happened to you?' Roberto Carlos teased. 'New hairstyle, new celebration – you used to be cool!'

Turkey were unlucky to lose to Brazil, but in the next game China stood no chance.

Roberto Carlos smashed a free kick rocket into the top corner. 1–0!

Rivaldo volleyed home Ronaldinho's cross. 2–0!

Ronaldo played a one-two with Ronaldinho. As he went to shoot, a defender pulled him back. Penalty! Ronaldinho stepped up and scored. 3–0!

Cafu gave Ronaldo an easy tap-in at the back-post. 4–0!

At the final whistle, Roberto Carlos walked happily over to his fellow goalscorers. 'See guys, I told you. We're the *4* Rs!'

With back-to-back wins, Brazil were through to the next round. Surely, the last group match would be a good chance to rest the biggest stars? Ronaldo didn't see it that way, however.

'Please don't drop me!' he begged Scolari. 'I'm just finding my rhythm. I need game-time, remember!'

His manager gave in and after fifteen minutes against Costa Rica, Ronaldo was already on a hat-trick. Both goals were as much about strength as skill. Twice, he shrugged off defenders and then nutmegged the goalkeeper.

'There's nothing I love more than a World Cup!' Ronaldo cheered as he jumped into Gilberto Silva's arms.

Many football fans had written him off as a fading hero, but with goal after goal, he was proving them wrong. Ronaldo was still the best, most complete striker around.

The spirit in the Brazilian squad was sky high. On

the team bus, Ronaldinho played the samba drums, and everyone danced and sang along. Not only were they winning matches, but they were also playing 'o jogo bonito' – 'The Beautiful Game'. The Brazilian people loved their entertaining football and so did the rest of the world.

Against Belgium, they took their flair to the next level. Ronaldinho cut inside and played an incredible pass with the outside of his right foot. On the edge of the penalty area, Rivaldo chested the ball down and smashed a swerving shot into the top corner. 1–0!

The stadium in Japan went wild. On the touchline, Scolari hugged his coaches and on the pitch, the players hugged Rivaldo.

Brazil still needed another goal to make the victory safe, and Ronaldo was determined to score it. Kléberson raced down the right wing and delivered a brilliant cross. He had time to take a touch, but he didn't need it. Instead, Ronaldo shot first time and nutmegged yet another goalkeeper.

Goooooooooooooooooooooaaaaaaaaaaaaaaaaalllllllllllll llllllllllllllll!!!!!!!!!!!!!!!!!!!!

It was his fifth goal of the tournament, one ahead of Rivaldo and one ahead of his total in 1998.

'And I've still got three more games to go!' he told Scolari. Ronaldo was totally focused on reaching his third World Cup final.

In the quarter-final against England, Brazil were losing 1–0 until Ronaldinho came to the rescue. He set up Rivaldo for the equaliser and then scored an amazing free kick to win the game.

The 'Third R', Ronaldo, was quieter than usual and he only lasted seventy minutes. At the final whistle, he raised both arms in the air and went back out onto the pitch to congratulate his teammates.

'Don't worry, I'm just saving myself for the final!' he joked.

First, however, Brazil had a semi-final to get through. They had already beaten Turkey 2–1 in the group stage but now they faced them again, and this time, it was going to be much tougher. Their defence was solid, and they had good attacking players too.

'Don't underestimate them!' Scolari told his players firmly.

Ronaldo nodded from experience. He played with Emre Belözoğlu, Hakan Şükür and Okan Buruk at Inter Milan. They were more than capable of pulling off a huge World Cup upset.

With Ronaldinho suspended, Ronaldo knew that he needed to up his game. With Rivaldo's help, he had to unlock Turkey's tight defence but at half-time, it was still 0–0.

'This is when we *really* need you!' Scolari told his star striker, looking him straight in the eyes.

That was a lot of pressure to cope with, but Ronaldo was used to it. He just needed a moment – a moment of magic.

Gilberto Silva passed to Ronaldo on the left. There were two defenders in front of him, but by moving the ball from left foot to right foot, he skipped straight through them. He was into the penalty area now, with another four opponents surrounding him. What would he do next?

Sadly, it wasn't the right time for one of Ronaldo's wondergoals, where he dribbled round everyone. It was the World Cup semi-final and he couldn't waste this opportunity by going for glory. Brazil just needed a goal – any goal.

Ronaldo didn't pull his left leg back and shoot with all his power. Instead, he poked the ball cleverly with the outside of his right foot. It caught the Turkey goalkeeper by surprise and bobbled up over his outstretched arm and into the bottom corner.

Goooooooooooooooooooaaaaaaaaaaaaaaaaaallllllllllll lllllllllllllll!!!!!!!!!!!!!!!!!!!!!

Ronaldo wagged his finger and then stood in front of the fans, with his arms out wide. Despite all the doubts, he hadn't let Brazil down. Instead, he had led them all the way to another World Cup Final.

And he saved his best performance for last. Against Germany, Ronaldo scored both goals in a 2–0 win. The first was a simple rebound from Rivaldo's strike but the second was classic Ronaldo. In the penalty area, he calmly controlled the ball and then placed a powerful shot into the bottom corner.

Goooooooooooooooooooaaaaaaaaaaaaaaaaaallllllllllll lllllllllllllll!!!!!!!!!!!!!!!!!!!!!

He wagged his finger again and again until it started to hurt.

'Ronaldo to the rescue!' Roberto Carlos laughed.

It felt so good to finally be Brazil's World Cup hero, after the frustration of 1994 and the disappointment of 1998. Even after two years of injury, Ronaldo had bounced back to become 'The Phenomenon' once more.

When it was his turn to hold the golden trophy, he studied it carefully before he kissed it. It was the best day of his life and he wanted to enjoy it for as long as possible. Finally, it was time for the moment he'd been waiting for. He lifted the trophy high above his head and roared.

Ronaldo returned to a hero's welcome in Brazil. Not only did he have his second World Cup winners' medal, but he also had the Golden Boot for the tournament's top goalscorer and the Silver Ball award for the second-best player.

'Not bad for a month's work!' Ronaldo joked.

CHAPTER 18

THE NEW GALÁCTICO

After his amazing performances at the 2002 World Cup, Ronaldo was back where he belonged, as the hottest property in football. He was keen to leave Inter Milan and start over somewhere new, but where? Which clubs wanted him, which clubs could afford him, and which clubs would give him lots of game-time?

Manchester United, Arsenal and AC Milan were all interested, but Ronaldo preferred the weather and style of football in Spain. Although Barcelona were keen to re-sign him, Ronaldo decided that he needed a fresh challenge. That only left one major option – Real Madrid.

Their ambitious president Florentino Pérez had been building a team of top superstars to kick off an exciting new *Galáctico* era at the club. It was a project that really interested Ronaldo, especially as Real had just won the Champions League.

'I really want to win that trophy!' he told his agent.

His old Barcelona teammate Luís Figo was already there, and so was his 1998 World Cup Final rival Zinedine Zidane. And best of all, Ronaldo would be able to team up with his best friend, Roberto Carlos, for club as well as country.

'Come join me in Madrid!' Roberto urged Ronaldo. 'We'll have so much fun together.'

Ronaldo was ready to go but the talks between Inter Milan and Real Madrid dragged on and on, all the way through August 2002 and into September.

'The Spanish season is about to start!' he moaned to his agent. 'What's taking so long?'

Just before the transfer deadline, the deal was finally done. Ronaldo became the new *Galáctico* for £30 million. When he arrived at the Bernabéu

Stadium, he posed for photos with the club president.

'This is a great day for Real Madrid!' Pérez told the media happily.

What shirt would Ronaldo wear? His favourite Number 9 was already taken by Fernando Morientes. Raúl was Number 7, Steve McManaman was Number 8, and Luís was Number 10.

'Number 11 it is, then!' Ronaldo decided without a fuss. No matter what shirt he wore, he was there to score lots and lots of goals.

Ronaldo couldn't wait to get started at Real. With so many familiar faces at the training ground, it didn't take him long to settle in.

'I've missed your crosses!' he told Luís as they hugged.

'And I've missed your goals!' the Portuguese winger replied.

Ronaldo was a substitute for Real Madrid's match against Alavés. His new manager wanted to ease him in gently. 'I'll bring you on for the last twenty to thirty minutes,' Vicente del Bosque promised.

The striker smiled. 'Thanks Boss, that's plenty of

time for me to grab a few goals on my debut!'

The atmosphere was nice and relaxed as the players entered the dressing room before the match. With a team stuffed full of superstars, Real Madrid had every reason to feel very confident.

'Don't worry,' Zinedine joked with Ronaldo, 'we'll make sure we're winning comfortably by the time you come on. You'll be able to take it easy!'

Roberto Carlos passed to Zinedine, who curled the ball into the top corner. 1–0!

Luís stepped up to take a penalty and sent the keeper the wrong way. 2–0!

On the bench, Ronaldo clapped and smiled. 'I think I'm going to enjoy playing with these guys!' he said to himself.

Although their opponents pulled one goal back, finally, Ronaldo's big moment arrived. As he ran onto the field, the Real Madrid fans stood up and cheered his name. Could he produce the same kind of magic that he had shown for Brazil at the World Cup? They couldn't wait to see what he would do.

They only had to wait one minute. When Roberto

Carlos crossed the ball from the left, Ronaldo chested the ball down and fired it straight past the keeper. 3–1!

Goooooooooooooooooooaaaaaaaaaaaaaaaaalllllllllllll llllllllllllll!!!!!!!!!!!!!!!!!!!!

'Wow, welcome to the team!' Zinedine shouted as all the players jumped on their new star.

It was party time at the Bernabéu. Luís beat the offside trap and chipped the ball cheekily over the keeper with the outside of his right foot. 4–1!

Steve dribbled forward and laid the ball across to Ronaldo. His shot flew past the diving goalkeeper and the sliding defenders too. 5–1!

What a start! At his new club Real Madrid, Ronaldo was off the mark in style.

'What's your target for this season?' a journalist asked him after the match.

'I'm going to score twenty-five league goals!' Ronaldo announced confidently.

That was a very bold claim of Ronaldo's; halfway through the season, he was still stuck on eight goals. He needed to up his game and so did Real Madrid.

They were five points behind Real Sociedad at the top of La Liga.

'What a waste of money!' some fans chanted at Ronaldo.

He was determined to prove them wrong, just like he had proved everyone wrong at the World Cup. Eventually, slowly but surely, Ronaldo's partnership with Raúl came to life.

In *El Clásico* against Barcelona, Raúl jumped and flicked the ball on for Ronaldo to chase. With a burst of pace, he got there first. Inside the penalty area, Ronaldo slowed down and waited for the ball to bounce, before shooting through the goalkeeper's legs. Nutmeg!

Gooooooooooooooooooooaaaaaaaaaaaaaaaaaalllllllllllll llllllllllllllll!!!!!!!!!!!!!!!!!!!!

Ronaldo was relieved to score such an important goal for his club. 'Hopefully, the fans will like me more after that!' he thought to himself.

With four games to go, Ronaldo was up to seventeen goals that season, but Real Madrid were still a point behind Real Sociedad. All they could do was keep winning and hope that their rivals slipped up.

Away at Valencia, Zinedine played the corner short to Luís, who curled the ball right onto Ronaldo's head.

Goooooooooooooooooooaaaaaaaaaaaaaaaaalllllllllllll lllllllllllllll!!!!!!!!!!!!!!!!!!!!!

In the second half, Real Madrid passed the ball around patiently, waiting for the right time to set Ronaldo free. With the outside of his right foot, Luís picked out his teammate's run perfectly. Ronaldo brought the ball down beautifully, dribbled round the goalkeeper and scored again.

Watching goals like that, the Real Madrid fans changed their mind about Ronaldo. When he scored two more against local rivals Atlético Madrid, they even started cheering his name.

Ronaldo! Ronaldo! Ronaldo!

The supporters grew even louder at full-time. 'What's going on?' Ronaldo wondered.

'Sociedad lost!' Roberto Carlos explained with a big smile on his face.

That meant that if Real Madrid could beat Athletic Bilbao, they would be crowned Champions of Spain.

In his second season at PSV, Ronaldo had finished second in the Dutch league. In his one season at Barcelona, Ronaldo had finished second in the Spanish league. In his first season at Inter Milan, he had finished second in the Italian league. It was time to change that record by finishing first for once.

Luís fed the ball to Roberto Carlos as he galloped down the left wing. His cross was a little behind Ronaldo, but he managed to stretch and guide it into the net. 1–0!

Goooooooooooooooooooaaaaaaaaaaaaaaaalllllllllllll llllllllllllll!!!!!!!!!!!!!!!!!!!

Ronaldo ran towards his best friend, pointing and smiling. Roberto Carlos did the same and jumped up into Ronaldo's arms. 'The title is nearly ours!' he screamed.

Athletic Bilbao pulled level but not for long. Roberto Carlos scored a ferocious free-kick and then Zinedine played Ronaldo through on goal. In the box, the Brazilian was lethal. He didn't even take a touch to control the ball before striking it past the keeper. 3–1!

Goooooooooooooooooooaaaaaaaaaaaaaaaalllllllllllll llllllllllllllll!!!!!!!!!!!!!!!!!!!

This time, the fans didn't just cheer Ronaldo's name. They stood up in their seats and clapped him too. He had won their support by doing what he did best – scoring big, important goals.

Ronaldo ended the season with twenty-three of those goals, two short of his target. But who cared? He finally had a European league winners' medal.

CHAPTER 19

CHASING CHAMPIONS LEAGUE GLORY

Away days in the Champions League were so exciting. Ronaldo got to travel all over Europe, playing football in Austria, Russia, Greece, Belgium and Germany.

In 2003, Real Madrid made it through to the quarter-finals, where they faced Manchester United. It would be Ronaldo's first-ever match at 'The Theatre of Dreams', Old Trafford. With Real 3–1 up after the first leg, he was determined to enjoy his English adventure.

'Let's do what we do best – attack!' Luís told his fellow Galácticos.

As Guti got the ball in midfield, Ronaldo was

already on the run towards goal. The through-ball was perfect. Ronaldo won the sprint race against United's defender Rio Ferdinand. In his head, he considered his two options:

1) cut inside and dribble past Ferdinand

or

2) shoot straight away

He chose the second option. From the edge of the penalty area, his shot swerved and dipped under the goalkeeper's arms.

Goooooooooooooooooooaaaaaaaaaaaaaaaaalllllllllllll llllllllllllllll!!!!!!!!!!!!!!!!!!!!!

Old Trafford was silent, apart from the one stand of screaming Real Madrid supporters. With one incredible strike, Ronaldo had blown away United's last hopes of victory. They would now need to score four goals and the Brazilian was only just getting started.

Ronaldo was a man on a mission. He had won the Cup Winners' Cup and the UEFA Cup with Barcelona and Inter Milan but now he was chasing Champions League glory. It was always a bad idea to try to stand in his way.

Early in the second–half, Zinedine passed to Roberto Carlos, who crossed to Ronaldo for an easy tap-in. It was another great Galáctico goal.

'I'm on a hat-trick!' Ronaldo cried out.

A few minutes later, he got the ball from Luís and attacked at speed. He had options to his left and options to his right, but there was no way that he was going to pass. Instead, as the United defenders backed away in fear, Ronaldo took a shot. There was only one possible end to the story...

Goooooooooooooooooooooaaaaaaaaaaaaaaaaaallllllllllll llllllllllllllll!!!!!!!!!!!!!!!!!!!!!

What a strike and what a way to complete his hat-trick! Ronaldo ran towards the corner and punched the air. He was really enjoying his trip to Old Trafford.

With twenty-five minutes to go, Del Bosque gave his star striker a well-deserved rest. As Ronaldo left the pitch, the stadium filled with the sound of clapping, from both the Real Madrid fans *and* the Manchester United fans. His striking masterclass had been that good.

'You just can't prepare for someone as special as Ronaldo,' the United manager Sir Alex Ferguson admitted afterwards.

Next up was a semi-final against Italian giants Juventus. Ronaldo opened the scoring at the Bernabéu with another composed finish. With their star striker on fire, Real Madrid were on their way to a second Champions League final in a row. They won the first leg 2–1, but there was bad news.

Ronaldo was used to Juventus's tough tackling after his days at Inter Milan. He tried to stay away from trouble but just before half-time, Mark Iuliano crashed into the back of his legs. If he couldn't stop him fairly, the defender was going to foul him.

'Argggghhhhh!' Ronaldo screamed out in agony.

Slowly, he got back to his feet, but his right leg was still painful.

'Are you okay to continue?' Roberto Carlos asked his friend.

Ronaldo nodded and winced, but he was soon substituted. Del Bosque wanted to protect his star striker for the trip to Italy. Unfortunately, Ronaldo wasn't fit enough to start in the second leg. By the time he came on in the second half, Real Madrid were already 2–0 down. He did his best, but he couldn't rescue his team this time.

'I *really* hate Juventus!' Ronaldo shouted in frustration. They had robbed him of the Italian League title in 1998 and 2002, and now they had robbed him of his Champions League glory too.

'Hey, we'll come back even stronger next year,' Roberto Carlos said, trying to comfort his devastated teammate.

For the 2003–04 season, Ronaldo came back stronger, and fitter too. He was wearing his favourite Number 9 shirt again and he was scoring goals for fun.

In the Madrid Derby against Atlético, he took the kick-off with Raúl. The ball went back to new Galáctico David Beckham, who passed to Zinedine, who passed to Roberto Carlos. A few seconds later, the ball was back at Ronaldo's feet.

He was a long way from goal, but he pretended to take a long-range shot. As a defender slid in for the block, Ronaldo slipped the ball through his legs and burst into the penalty area. The Atlético players could only watch in shock as he flicked the ball over their diving goalkeeper.

Gooooooooooooooooooooaaaaaaaaaaaaaaaaalllllllllllll lllllllllllllll!!!!!!!!!!!!!!!!!!!!!

After just fourteen seconds, Real Madrid were already 1–0 up! The fans went wild, swinging their white scarves above their heads.

'Slow down Ronie, there's still ninety minutes to go!' Zinedine laughed as he chased after his teammate.

Ronaldo was enjoying his La Liga form, but his focus was still on Champions League glory. Real Madrid got through the group stages and took on Bayern Munich in the second round. It was Round Two of Ronaldo vs Germany goalkeeper Oliver Kahn.

In Munich, Ronaldo received the ball with his back to goal. As he flicked it on, a Bayern player fouled him. Free kick! Roberto Carlos took it and fired the ball around the wall. Ronaldo had to jump to get out of the way and it squirmed through the goalkeeper's hands. 1–1! Ronaldo pumped his fists. Poor Kahn had made another costly mistake against him.

At the Bernabéu, Zinedine scored to send Real Madrid through to the quarter-finals again. This time, however, that's where their journey ended, as Monaco beat them.

Ronaldo kept chasing Champions League glory, but it slipped further and further away from him. In 2005, Real Madrid lost to Juventus again in the second round. In 2006, they lost to Arsenal at the same stage.

'I suppose I can't win everything,' Ronaldo told Roberto, 'but we strikers are greedy!'

'Tell me about it!' his best friend laughed.

CHAPTER 20

WORLD CUP 2006: THE MAGIC QUARTET

Ronaldo counted down the days until 9 June 2006 – it was World Cup time again! Brazil had the chance to become the first country to win the 'Hexa' – six World Cup trophies. After 1994 and 2002, Ronaldo also had the chance to complete his own hat-trick. Could Brazil defend their title in Germany?

'Of course, we can!' Ronaldo told Roberto Carlos.

With Rivaldo's retirement, the 'Three Rs' era was over. Now, it was all about 'The Magic Quartet' – Ronaldo and Ronaldinho, plus playmaker Kaká and striker Adriano. It was another exciting Brazilian line-up.

At twenty-nine, Ronaldo was now one of the

senior players in the squad. He was also in
good form for his country, scoring ten goals in
qualification. This was now his fourth World Cup,
so he had lots of experience to pass on to his
younger teammates.

'Slow and steady wins the race,' Ronaldo told his
strike partner Adriano. 'If all goes according to plan,
we've got seven games ahead of us!'

Brazil's first match against Croatia was a frustrating
one for Ronaldo. With so many attackers on the
pitch, he hardly had a touch, let alone a shot.
Fortunately, Kaká's screamer got them off to a
winning start.

Ronaldo didn't score against Australia either, but
at least he had a better game. On the edge of the
penalty area, three defenders surrounded him, trying
to stop his stepovers. That left Adriano in space on
the right and Ronaldo gave him a simple chance to
score. 1–0!

Their back-up striker, Fred, came off the bench to
grab the second goal. Ronaldo had been his country's
goalscoring hero in the past but that didn't mean his

MATT AND TOM OLDFIELD

place was safe. Back home in Brazil, lots of people thought Ronaldo should be dropped from the team.

'Right, I really need to prove that I can still score goals,' he told himself.

In the first half against Japan, Ronaldo kept shooting and the goalkeeper kept saving. He tried to stay patient but when Japan took the lead, he knew he had to do something quickly. Ronaldinho crossed to Cicinho, who headed the ball to Ronaldo, who headed the ball past the goalkeeper.

Goooooooooooooooooooaaaaaaaaaaaaaaaaalllllllllll llllllllllllll!!!!!!!!!!!!!!!!!!

Finally! It wasn't one of Ronaldo's trademark wondergoals, but he was off the mark and his finger was wagging once more.

'Go get another!' Kaká told him.

Suddenly, Brazil rediscovered 'The Beautiful Game'. They raced into a 3–1 lead and Ronaldo wasn't done yet. After a one-two with Robinho, he found enough space to curl a beautiful shot into the bottom corner.

Ronaldo was back but he still wasn't satisfied. 'I

should have got at least a hat-trick tonight. I could
have scored six or seven!'

Adriano laughed. 'We've still got four games to
go. Remember what you told me, Ronie? Slow and
steady wins the race!'

In the knockout stages of the World Cup, Ronaldo
wasn't at all slow against Ghana. In the fifth
minute, he raced on to Kaká's through-ball, beat the
goalkeeper with a stepover and tapped the ball into
the net.

*Goooooooooooooooooooooaaaaaaaaaaaaaaaalllllllllllll
lllllllllllllll!!!!!!!!!!!!!!!!!!!!*

It was a very special moment for Ronaldo. With his
fifteenth World Cup goal, he was now the top scorer
in the tournament's history.

'Congratulations!' Kaká shouted, giving him a big
hug.

'Once again, Ronaldo is the best player in the
world,' his manager Carlos Alberto Parreira said after
the match.

Ronaldo was pleased with his new record but
what he really wanted was that third World Cup

trophy. Brazil looked strong as they cruised into the quarter-finals, but they would need to be at their best for the big game against France. It was a replay of the 1998 World Cup Final, and Ronaldo wanted revenge.

'We can't lose to them again!' captain Cafu told his teammates in the dressing room.

Before kick-off, Ronaldo looked as relaxed as ever. He joked around with Ronaldinho and his Real Madrid friends, Zinedine Zidane and Claude Makélélé.

After kick-off, however, Ronaldo's smile disappeared. He had a battle to win. As Ronaldinho's free kick flew towards him, Ronaldo jumped high, but he couldn't direct his header down.

'Next time!' Ronaldinho shouted, giving him a big thumbs-up.

Would there be a next time? As well as Zinedine and Claude, France also had Thierry Henry, one of the top strikers in the world. He was younger and quicker than Ronaldo, but when it came to big games and big goals, the Brazilian was still the best in the business. Or was he?

The entire nation prayed for one of his moments of magic, but it was Zinedine who was running the show for France. He crossed the ball to Henry who volleyed it in at the back post.

Disaster! Brazil were losing, and they needed their superstar more than ever.

'Keep going!' the fans cheered him on.

Ronaldo dribbled into the France penalty area but then stumbled to the floor.

Tick-tock!

Ronaldo found the space to shoot but he dragged it wide.

Tick-tock!

Ronaldo dropped deep and then weaved his way through the French midfield. It took a foul to stop him. Free kick! It was in a good position, but Ronaldinho's strike flew just over the bar.

Tick-tock!

In the dying seconds, Ronaldo had one last chance. He struck his shot well but not well enough to beat France's goalkeeper Fabien Barthez.

Tick-tock!

It was over. Brazil were out of the 2006 World Cup, beaten by France once again.

The smile was back on Zinedine's face, but not Ronaldo's. He was so devastated that he walked straight off the pitch.

Was this the end of his amazing international career? It was a sad way to say goodbye, but could Ronaldo really make it to one more tournament in 2010? His mind said yes but his body said no. At twenty-nine years old, he had already played so much football.

'We'll have to wait and see,' Ronaldo told the Brazilian people.

First, he needed to put his World Cup woe behind him. Ronaldo was off on a second Italian adventure.

CHAPTER 21

AC MILAN

'Are you sure about this?' his agent asked him.

Ronaldo had received an offer from the other big club in Milan – AC – and he wanted to accept it.

'If I can play for Barcelona and Real Madrid, then surely I can play for Inter and AC Milan too!' he argued.

'You know Inter and AC share a stadium, right?' his agent continued.

'Trust me, it'll be fine. My time at Inter was ages ago!' Ronaldo reassured him with his famous toothy smile. 'Right now, I just want to play regular first-team football again.'

His time at Real Madrid had really run out of

steam. The Galáctico era was over, with Luís joining
Inter and Zinedine retiring after the World Cup. The
new manager, Fabio Capello, wasn't interested in
superstars. He wanted a solid, reliable striker and
so he signed Ruud van Nistelrooy from Manchester
United.

That left Ronaldo in his least favourite position of
all – on the bench.

'Goalscorers need game-time,' he complained to
Roberto Carlos. 'It's all about confidence!'

He didn't really suit the super sub role, but against
Athletic Bilbao, Ronaldo saved Real Madrid. They
were losing 1–0 when he came on at half-time.
As Sergio Ramos's long ball came towards him, he
plucked it perfectly out of the air before nutmegging
the keeper.

*Goooooooooooooooooooooaaaaaaaaaaaaaaaalllllllllllll
llllllllllllll!!!!!!!!!!!!!!!!!!!*

At his best, Ronaldo made football look so easy. It
was a great reminder of his incredible natural talent.
Real Madrid's loss would be AC Milan's gain.

When he arrived in Italy in early 2007, Ronaldo

received a warm welcome from his international teammates, Dida, Cafu and Kaká. The club's Brazilian gang was growing.

'Bem vinda!' they cheered in Portuguese.

Filippo Inzaghi already wore the Number 9 shirt for AC Milan, so Ronaldo chose the next best thing – Number 99!

'You always have to stand out, don't you!' Kaká laughed.

AC Milan were still in the Champions League, but Ronaldo was cup-tied because he had already played for Real Madrid earlier in the season. He focused instead on grabbing as many goals as possible in the Italian League.

Ronaldo didn't score on his debut, but he did score on his first start for AC Milan. Before the match, his new manager Carlo Ancelotti was worried about the striker's fitness. 'Are you sure you're ready for playing ninety minutes?' he asked.

Ronaldo laughed. 'Trust me, if I play, I will score!'

After fifteen minutes, Andrea Pirlo chipped a cross towards the back post. Ronaldo jumped and steered a powerful header into the corner of the net.

Goooooooooooooooooooaaaaaaaaaaaaaaaalllllllllllll lllllllllllllll!!!!!!!!!!!!!!!!!!!!!!

He still had the golden, goalscoring touch. Ronaldo hugged Andrea and grinned. 'With passes like that, how can I miss?'

So many of Ronaldo's goals came either at the beginning or the end of matches. Against Siena, he scored in both. With ten minutes to go, Kaká dribbled into the box and pulled the ball back for an easy finish.

'Thanks!' Ronaldo called out, jumping into his teammate's arms.

'Careful, you're heavy!' Kaká groaned.

'Shut up, you sound like Ancelotti!'

At the final whistle, the AC Milan supporters had a new hero. Ronaldo became even more of a fans' favourite when he scored in the derby against Inter. It was a classic 'Phenomenon' strike. He dribbled forward until the defenders closed in, and then unleashed a rocket of a shot into the bottom corner. His accuracy was unbelievable.

Gooooooooooooooooooooaaaaaaaaaaaaaaaaallllllllllll lllllllllllllll!!!!!!!!!!!!!!!!!!!!

The San Siro Stadium was stunned but they shouldn't have been surprised. Inter knew exactly what Ronaldo could do with the ball at his feet. He wagged his finger and then put his hands to his ears. That goal would teach the Inter fans not to boo him next time.

Unfortunately, AC Milan lost the match 2–1. Their players were all focusing on the Champions League. All of them except Ronaldo. He finished the season with seven Serie A goals, but his teammates finished as the Champions of Europe. He couldn't help feeling jealous.

'Real won the Spanish League and AC won the Champions League,' he moaned to Kaká. 'I played for both teams this season but what have I won? Absolutely nothing!'

'Sorry, are two World Cups and two Ballon d'Ors not enough for you?'

'I was talking about this season!'

Ronaldo had high hopes for the 2007–08 season

and so did the AC Milan fans. They had a new all-Brazilian attack to enjoy – Ronaldo, Kaká and the new kid on the block, Alexandre Pato. They had a nickname before they'd even kicked a ball together – 'Ka–Pa–Ro'.

'Catchy!' Kaká laughed.

'I like it but why is my name last?' Ronaldo joked. 'I'm the senior player here. How old are you, Pato – twelve?'

'Ka–Pa–Ro' made their debut against Napoli, and Ronaldo celebrated by scoring another early goal. After collecting Andrea's clever pass, he turned and shot. The ball bounced up off the keeper's legs and over the goal line, with a bit of help from Pato. 1–0!

'You better not be claiming that goal, kid,' Ronaldo called out with a smile. 'It's mine!'

'No, you can have it. I'll score a better one of my own!' Pato replied cheekily.

Before he could do that, however, Ronaldo scored again with a diving header.

Goooooooooooooooooooooaaaaaaaaaaaaaaaaalllllllllllll llllllllllllllll!!!!!!!!!!!!!!!!!!!!

It was turning out to be a very special day, and it got even better when Kaká made it 4–2 and then Pato made it 5–2. AC Milan's Brazilians were just too hot to handle.

Sadly, Ronaldo's season was soon over. Against Livorno in February 2008, he jumped for a header, as normal but as his left foot landed, he heard and felt the SNAP!

Ronaldo lay on the grass, screaming and screaming. It had happened again. First his right knee against Lazio and now his left knee against Livorno. It was the same sad story again. Ronaldo left the pitch on a stretcher, his hand hiding the tears.

He didn't know it then, but his second Italian adventure was over before he'd won a single trophy.

CHAPTER 22

CORINTHIANS AND GOODBYE

As he recovered from the third bad knee injury of his career, Ronaldo travelled back to the place where he felt the happiest – his homeland. During his time in Europe, he had returned to Brazil as often as his clubs would let him. He missed the food, the weather, the music and, of course, the parties.

'It's great to be back!' Ronaldo told his friends and family.

As soon as he could walk without crutches, he started working hard at Flamengo, the team that he had supported as a child in Rio de Janeiro. At first, Ronaldo stayed in the gym, building up his leg strength, but eventually, he joined the players on the training ground.

'Look who's back!' his old international teammate Adriano joked. He was now Flamengo's star striker. 'Are you here to take my place?'

Ronaldo laughed. 'One step at a time, mate. I'm not as young as I used to be!'

He hadn't yet made a decision about his foot-balling future. He knew that he wanted to stay in Brazil but at which club? There were lots of teams to choose from.

In the end, Ronaldo chose Corinthians in São Paulo. 'I'm still a professional footballer and I still like big challenges,' he explained to the media. 'I think this challenge is going to be excellent for me.'

Fifteen years after leaving Cruzeiro to join PSV, Ronaldo was back in Brazilian football. He felt relaxed and excited at the same time. Did he still have that golden, goalscoring touch? There was only one way to find out.

Ronaldo's first game passed without a goal but right at the end of his second game, he lost his marker and popped up at the back post to score a header.

Goooooooooooooooooooaaaaaaaaaaaaaaaaallllllllllll llllllllllllllllll!!!!!!!!!!!!!!!!!!!!

Ronaldo had lost his speed, but he hadn't lost his striker's instinct. He still knew how to be in the right place at the right time to score.

In his delight, Ronaldo jumped over the advertising boards and climbed up onto the fence to celebrate with the Corinthians fans. The crowd went wild, so wild that the fence fell down!

It was a dream start for Ronaldo and he didn't stop there. He kept on scoring, and Corinthians kept on winning. They made it all the way to two big finals.

In the São Paulo final, Corinthians faced Pelé's old team, Santos. They had a new teenage superstar called Neymar Jr but that night, a Brazilian legend taught him a lesson. Chicão scored first with a brilliant free kick but after that, it was The Ronaldo Show.

Ronaldo brought down the long pass beautifully,

like his foot was a ball magnet. The poor Santos goalkeeper had no chance of stopping 'The Phenomenon'. *Bang* – 2–0!

Ronaldo ran onto Elias's pass, but he no longer had the pace to keep going towards goal. Instead, he cut inside with a clever flick and then chipped the ball over the goalkeeper's head. *3–1!*

Gooooooooooooooooooooaaaaaaaaaaaaaaaaalllllllllllll lllllllllllllll!!!!!!!!!!!!!!!!!!!!

It was a wondergoal worthy of winning any final. Ronaldo jogged away with his finger wagging and a huge smile on his face. He was born for the big time. He just loved being the hero.

In the Brazil Cup final, Corinthians faced Internacional. The stage was set for yet another big Ronaldo goal. Elias's quick free-kick curled perfectly into his path. Despite all the knee injuries and fitness problems, Ronaldo still beat the centre-back in the race to the ball.

In the penalty area, he always knew what to do. Ronaldo cut in on his left foot and then fooled the keeper at his near post.

Gooooooooooooooooooooaaaaaaaaaaaaaaaallllllllllll llllllllllllll!!!!!!!!!!!!!!!!!!!!!

Ronaldo ran to the fans and threw his arms up in the air. The Corinthians season was just getting better and better.

'I should have come back to Brazil years ago!' he joked with Elias.

Many people thought that Ronaldo had only returned to football for the money. But with two trophies and twenty-three goals, he had proved them wrong. He had returned to football for the glory.

Ronaldo kissed the cup and lifted it high above his head as he danced the night away with his teammates.

Campeones, Campeones, Olé! Olé! Olé!

After that amazing first season, Ronaldo thought about stopping, but he didn't want to. He loved playing football and he loved entertaining the fans.

'As long as I'm still having fun and scoring goals, I'll carry on!' Ronaldo told Roberto Carlos, who had just joined him at Corinthians.

'We better go have some fun then!' his friend replied.

Against São Paulo, they both stood over the free kick. It was a long way out, so Ronaldo let Roberto Carlos take it. The left-back pumped his powerful legs and thundered the ball through the wall and past the goalkeeper too. GOAL!

'Nice strike,' Ronaldo cheered, 'but I'll be taking the next one!'

He was still having fun, but the goals were starting to dry up. Plus, each game was hurting more and more. In February 2011, Ronaldo decided it was finally time to retire.

It was a very sad day for football. The 'Boy from Bento Ribeiro' had enjoyed an amazing career, in the Netherlands, Spain, Italy and, of course, his beloved Brazil. The superstar striker was leaving the beautiful game with so many memories, trophies and goals.

'It's very hard to stop doing something that made me so happy,' Ronaldo told the world. 'My head wants to go on, but my body can't take any more. It's time to go.'

FINAL FAREWELL

São Paulo, 7 June 2011

Five years after his last game for Brazil's national team, Ronaldo was back to say a final farewell to the fans in a friendly match against Romania. It was going to be a very emotional night for the whole country. Brazil would never forget their hero from the 2002 World Cup.

Ronaldo came on after thirty minutes. By that time, Fred had already given Brazil a 1–0 lead, and he celebrated his goal with a finger wag in tribute to the man of the moment.

As the fourth official held up the Number 9 on his board, the supporters clapped and cheered. Fred walked off, smiling and bowing to Ronaldo. 'My hero!' he shouted.

A huge yellow banner spread across the stadium, showing his face and three words. 'PRA SEMPRE, FENOMENO' – 'FOREVER, PHENOMENON'.

Ronaldo jogged on to the field and took up his favourite position as his country's star striker. Brazil's Number 9 looked across at Brazil's new Number 10, Neymar Jr, and smiled.

'You're going to have to do all the running for me, kid. I'm old now!'

Neymar Jr smiled right back. 'No problem, I'll do my best to get you a farewell goal!'

His cross from the right rolled straight to Ronaldo in the six-yard box. This was it! It looked like an easy chance for the top scorer in World Cup history. The crowd got ready to dance... but the goalkeeper saved it.

'Noooo!' Ronaldo winced. 'Sorry guys, I'm a little rusty.'

A few minutes later, Neymar Jr set him up again. This time, Ronaldo skied his shot high over the bar.

'It's a good thing this is my final game!' he joked.

'No way, keep going!' Robinho called out, giving his friend a high-five.

Would Ronaldo be third time lucky? Neymar Jr pulled the ball back and he struck it powerfully... but the goalkeeper saved it again.

'Did no-one tell him it was my final farewell?' Ronaldo laughed. 'That guy's ruining my big day!'

The referee blew the half-time whistle, and his amazing international career was over. As Ronaldo left the pitch for the last time, the two teams formed a tunnel for him to walk through. He shook each player's hand and waved to the crowd.

It was a very special moment for Ronaldo. He had the match ball in his hand and his two sons at his side, Ronald and Alexander. After wrapping a Brazilian flag around his shoulders, it was time for The Phenomenon's farewell speech:

'I had chances to score tonight – sorry for not finishing them like I used to! Thanks for everything you've done during my career. When I cried, you cried with me. When I smiled, you smiled with me.

I'm so proud to be a Brazilian!'

And with that, Ronaldo retired. As well as being his country's second top scorer, behind Pelé, with sixty-two goals, he had won six international trophies – an Olympic Bronze medal, the FIFA Confederations Cup, two Copa Américas and, of course, two World Cups. That was a whole lot of joy to bring to one nation.

'Right, over to you, kid,' Ronaldo winked cheekily at Neymar Jr. 'Let's see how many World Cups *you* can win!'

Turn the page for a sneak preview of
another brilliant football story by
Matt and Tom Oldfield. . .

NEYMAR

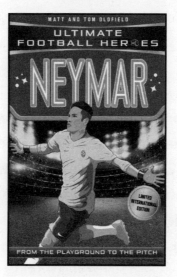

Available now!

CHAPTER 1

OLYMPIC GOLD

'We have to win!' Neymar Jr told his teammates. He
normally liked to laugh and dance before a match but
not this time. He was captain and this was serious.
'Let's get revenge for the 2014 World Cup!'

Neymar Jr was the only member of Brazil's 2016
Olympic squad who had also been there for that
awful night in Belo Horizonte two years earlier.
When Germany thrashed Brazil 7–1 in the semi-
finals on home soil, the whole nation was left
heartbroken. Football was their greatest passion.

But it hurt Neymar Jr more than most because
he was injured for that game and couldn't be the
national hero that they needed. This time, though, as

they faced Germany once again, he was fit and raring to go.

'Germany better watch out!' his strike partner, Gabriel Jesus cheered.

After a long season at Barcelona, Neymar Jr had taken a little while to find his form at the Olympics. As the one of the oldest players in the squad, his teammates depended on him. It was a lot of responsibility and after three matches, Neymar Jr hadn't scored a single goal.

'Don't worry,' the coach Rogério Micale told him. 'That was your warm-up; now we need you at your best in these next big games!'

Neymar Jr scored one against Colombia in the quarter-finals, then two against Honduras in the semi-finals. He had rediscovered his *ginga* rhythm, his Brazilian flair, just in time.

'That means you should score a hat-trick in the final!' his teammate Marquinhos joked.

'No pressure, then!' Neymar Jr replied with a smile on his face.

He led the players out on to the pitch to face

Germany at the Maracanã Stadium in Rio de Janeiro. Nearly 60,000 Brazilians had come to cheer on their country, wearing the famous yellow shirt and waving yellow-and-green flags. They were ready for a party, and the noise and colour were incredible.

Neymar Jr stood with his hand on his heart and sang the national anthem loudly. He was so proud to represent his nation and he was one win away from making everyone very happy. He couldn't wait.

Midway through the first half, Brazil won a free-kick just outside the penalty area. It was a perfect opportunity for Neymar Jr. He placed the ball down, stepped back and took a long, deep breath. Then he curled the ball powerfully towards the top corner. It was too quick and high for the goalkeeper to save. The shot hit the underside of the crossbar and bounced down into the back of the net.

Goooooooooooooooaaaaaaaaaaaaaaaaaaalllllllllllllllllllllllllll!!!!!!!!!!!!!!!!!!!!

Neymar Jr had always dreamed of scoring amazing goals in international finals. Now it was a reality and he would never forget the moment. All of his teammates ran over and jumped on him.

'You did it!' Gabriel shouted.

After the celebrations, Neymar Jr told the others to calm down and focus. 'We haven't won this yet – concentrate!'

Brazil defended well but after sixty minutes, Germany equalised. Neymar Jr had more work to do. He dribbled past one defender and then dropped in a clever Cruyff Turn to wrong-foot a second. It was magical skill and the crowd loved it. He now had the space to shoot. The ball swerved past the goalkeeper's outstretched arm but just wide of the post.

'So close!' Neymar Jr said to himself, putting his hands on his head.

Brazil attacked again and again but they couldn't find a winning goal, even after thirty minutes of extra-time. It was time for penalties.

'I'll take the last one,' Neymar Jr told Micale. He was determined to be the national hero this time.

After eight penalties, it was 4–4. When Brazil's goalkeeper Weverton saved the ninth spot-kick,

Neymar Jr had his golden chance. He walked from the halfway line towards the penalty spot with thousands of fans cheering his name.

He picked up the ball, kissed it and put it back down. As he waited for the referee's whistle, he tried to slow his heartbeat down. If he was too excited, he might kick it over the bar. He needed to be his normal, cool self.

As he ran up, he slowed down to try to make the German goalkeeper move early. The keeper dived low to the right and Neymar Jr put his shot high and to the left. As the ball went in, Neymar burst into tears of joy. He had led his country all the way to the Olympic Gold Medal for the first time ever. As he fell to his knees and thanked God, the other Brazil players ran to hug their hero.

'You always said that we could do it!' his teammate Luan shouted. 'Now it's carnival time!'

As Neymar Jr got back on his feet, he listened to the incredible noise of the Maracanã crowd. It was the best thing he had ever heard.

'Imagine what the atmosphere would have been

like if we'd made it to the World Cup final and won it in 2014!' Neymar Jr thought to himself, but it was time to forget about the pains of the past and move forward. Thanks to him, his country was back at the top of world football again.

'Thank you!' the coach Micale said to him, giving him the biggest hug of all.

He was still only twenty-four but Neymar Jr had already been Brazil's number one superstar for years. There was so much pressure on him but he refused to let his country down, even after moving to Spain to play for Barcelona.

Neymar Jr had Brazil to thank for everything: the love of his family and friends; the support of his coaches at Portuguesa Santista and Santos; and above all, the amazing skills that he had first developed in street football, beach football and *futsal* matches in São Paulo.

RONALDO
HONOURS

Cruzeiro

🏆 Brazil Cup: 1993

🏆 Campeonato Mineiro: 1994

Barcelona

🏆 Spanish Super Cup: 1996

🏆 Copa Del Rey: 1997

🏆 UEFA Cup Winners' Cup: 1997

Inter Milan

🏆 UEFA Cup: 1998

Real Madrid

- 🏆 La Liga: 2002–03, 2006–07
- 🏆 Intercontinental Cup: 2002
- 🏆 Spanish Super Cup: 2003

Corinthians

- 🏆 Campeonato Paulista: 2009
- 🏆 Copa do Brasil: 2009

Brazil

- 🏆 FIFA World Cup: 1994, 2002
- 🏆 Summer Olympic Games Bronze Medal: 1996
- 🏆 Copa América: 1997, 1999
- 🏆 FIFA Confederations Cup: 1997

Individual

- 🏆 Brazilian League Top Scorer: 1993–94
- 🏆 Dutch League Top Scorer: 1994–95
- 🏆 FIFA World Player of the Year: 1996, 1997, 2002
- 🏆 Spanish League Top Scorer: 1996–97, 2003–04
- 🏆 European Golden Boot: 1996–97

🏆 UEFA Cup Winners' Cup Top Goal Scorer: 96–97

🏆 Copa América All–Star Team: 1997, 1999

🏆 Ballon d'Or: 1997, 2002

🏆 Serie A Footballer of the Year: 1997–98

🏆 UEFA Club Footballer of the Year: 1997–98

🏆 FIFA World Cup Golden Ball: 1998

🏆 FIFA World Cup All–Star Team: 1998, 2002

🏆 Copa América Top Scorer: 1999

🏆 FIFA World Cup Golden Boot: 2002

🏆 Golden Foot Award: 2006

🏆 Campeonato Paulista Best Player: 2009

RONALDO

9 THE FACTS

NAME: Ronaldo Luís Nazário de Lima

DATE OF BIRTH: 18 September 1976

AGE: 41

PLACE OF BIRTH: Bento Ribeiro, Rio de Janeiro

NATIONALITY: Brazilian

BEST FRIEND: Roberto Carlos

CURRENT CLUB: Barcelona, Inter Milan, Real Madrid

POSITION: ST

THE STATS

Height (cm):	183
Club appearances:	518
Club goals:	352
Club trophies:	13
International appearances:	98
International goals:	62
International trophies:	4
Ballon d'Ors:	2

★ ★ ★ **HERO RATING: 94** ★ ★ ★

GREATEST MOMENTS

Type and search the web links to see the magic for yourself!

★ 1   7 NOVEMBER 1993, CRUZEIRO 6–0 BAHIA

https://www.youtube.com/watch?v=LRa3NQxaKms

When Ronaldo scored five brilliant goals on Brazilian TV, a new national star was born. He tore defences apart with his skill, strength and speed, and he was still only seventeen years old. Everyone was so excited, nicknaming Ronaldo 'O Fenomeno' ('The Phenomenon') and 'The New Pelé'. Soon, he was off to the World Cup with the Brazilian national team.

★ 2 12 OCTOBER 1996, COMPOSTELA 1–5 BARCELONA

https://www.youtube.com/watch?v=qE774yQX6uQ

In his one season at Barcelona, Ronaldo scored a club record of forty-seven goals. There were so many amazing strikes, but this one against Compostela was the best of the lot. Ronaldo won the ball on the halfway line and burst forward, dribbling past four defenders on his path to goal.

★ 3 30 JUNE 2002, BRAZIL 2–0 GERMANY

https://www.youtube.com/watch?v=O8dUhMGtUtw

It was third time lucky for Ronaldo in the World Cup Final. After watching from the bench in 1994, he then wasn't well enough to lead Brazil to victory in 1998. In 2002, however, he made things right with both goals against Germany. The first was a lucky rebound but the second was a perfectly placed shot.

4 — 23 APRIL 2003, MANCHESTER UNITED 4–3 REAL MADRID

https://www.youtube.com/watch?v=KoPlUSG-vcg

Ronaldo enjoyed four successful seasons as one of Real Madrid's Galácticos. Nothing said 'superstar striker' like this Champions League hat-trick at Old Trafford. Ronaldo wasn't as quick as he used to be, but his shooting was sharper than ever. Sadly, the Brazilian never won European football's biggest trophy.

5 — 26 APRIL 2009, CORINTHIANS 3–1 SANTOS

https://www.youtube.com/watch?v=YSZZabJ5hlc

When Ronaldo returned to Brazil, many people thought that his career was over. How wrong they were! He still had that golden, goalscoring touch, as he showed in this league final for Corinthians against Neymar Jr's Santos. His first goal was a classic Ronaldo nutmeg finish and the second was one of the cheekiest chips you'll ever see. Natural talent never goes away.

PLAY LIKE YOUR HEROES

ULTIMATE WING WIZARD: THE RONALDO WONDERGOAL

SEE IT HERE You Tube

https://www.youtube.com/watch?v=qE774yQX6uQ

STEP 1: First of all, you're going to need the ball. Hopefully, you've got Luís Figo to set you up but if not, you're going to have to go win it yourself.

Step 2: Once you have the ball, turn and attack at top speed.

Step 3: Use your strength to hold off any dirty defenders tugging at your shirt.

Step 4: Use your close control to protect the ball from any tough tackles.

Step 5: If in trouble, move the ball quickly from foot to foot. Your left is as brilliant as your right, so you'll keep your opponents guessing.

Step 6: Once you're in the penalty area, fake to shoot and then dribble round the goalkeeper, before passing the ball into the net – too easy!

TEST YOUR KNOWLEDGE

QUESTIONS

1. Who was Ronaldo named after?

2. Which team did Ronaldo support as a child and who was his favourite player?

3. What sport did Ronaldo play at Valquiere Tennis Club?

4. Ronaldo played at the 1994 World Cup – true or false?

5. Ronaldo followed in which Brazilian striker's footsteps when he went to PSV Eindhoven and then Barcelona?

6. Why was Ronaldo called 'Ronaldinho' early in his career?

7. Who did Ronaldo share a room with at the 1998 World Cup?

8. What number did Ronaldo wear at Real Madrid and why?

9. Which two fellow Brazilians played with Ronaldo in AC Milan's 'Ka-Pa-Ro' attack?

10. How many World Cups did Ronaldo go to with Brazil?

11. How many World Cup goals did Ronaldo score?

Answers below. . . No cheating!

1. *Ronaldo Valente, the doctor who delivered him in hospital*
2. *Flamengo and their Number 10, Zico* 3. *Futsal* 5. *False – Ronaldo went to the tournament in the USA, but he didn't play a single minute.*
5. *Romário* 6. *There was another, older Ronaldo in the Brazil squad – Ronaldo Guiaro* 7. *Roberto Carlos* 8. *He wore Number 11 because Number 9 was already taken, and so were 7, 8 and 10* 9. *Kaká and Alexandre Pato* 10. *Four – 1994, 1998, 2002 and 2006* 11. *Fifteen*

This summer, your favourite football heroes will pull on their country's colours to go head-to-head for the ultimate prize – the World Cup.

Celebrate by making sure you have six of the best Ultimate Football Heroes, now with limited edition international covers!

COMING 31 ST MAY